Buying and Selling Currency for Profit

Buying and Selling Currency for Profit

Robert Wolenik

Contemporary Books, Inc.
Chicago

Library of Congress Cataloging in Publication Data

Wolenik, Robert.
    Buying and selling currency for profit.

    Includes index.
    1. Foreign exchange.   2. Forward exchange.
3. Speculation.   I. Title.
HG3853.F6W64   332.4'5   79-51001
ISBN 0-8092-7452-3

Copyright © 1980, 1979 by Robert Wolenik
All rights reserved
Published by Contemporary Books, Inc.
180 North Michigan Avenue, Chicago, Illinois 60601
Manufactured in the United States of America
Library of Congress Catalog Card Number: 79-51001
International Standard Book Number: 0-8092-7452-3

Published simultaneously in Canada by
Beaverbooks
953 Dillingham Road
Pickering, Ontario L1W 1Z7
Canada

Contents

Preface   *vii*

1 There's money to be made in money   *1*

2 Money as a commodity   *9*

3 Productivity—how it determines money's value   *29*

4 Inflation—and how it affects currency rates   *48*

5 Balance of payments—how to use it as a currency indicator   *66*

6 Petrodollars—shifting wealth away   *82*

7 Anticipating trends   *89*

8 The Eurodollar trap   *94*

9 Tomorrow's currency winners, today   *117*

10 The currency futures game   *135*

11 Gold, silver, and other precious metal investments   *159*

12 Should you try collectible currency?   *176*

Appendix   *185*

Index   *193*

Preface

EVERY day across the world people buy and sell houses, wheat, oil, antiques, and even water, making money on the transactions. There is almost no commodity that can be named that is not bought and sold at some level for profit. And that includes money itself. All across Europe and in most advanced countries, governments, private banks, large and small businesses, and a sizable number of citizens regularly trade U.S. dollars, yen, Deutschemarks, Swiss francs, etc. Here in the United States, the federal government, many businesses, and most large financial institutions regularly buy and sell currency. (Even the U.S. government makes a profit at it now and then!) Why, then, does only the tiniest minority of U.S. citizens buy and sell currency?

There are many reasons. Some citizens feel it is unpatriotic to do so. (We'll see in the course of this book that patriotism has almost nothing to do with currency investing.) Others would like to become involved in money trading, but simply don't know where and how to begin. And still others aren't even aware that it's possible to do it.

It is possible to make money buying and selling money here in the United States and, if you plan well and have some luck, it's possible to make a considerable profit. The investment required tends to be smaller than for many other fields and the potential for profit (and loss) tends to be greater.

The goal of this book is to bring the currency exchange field out into the open—to make it accessible to the little investor in the same way it has always been accessible to the big one. This book will show you how, every day, people are making money by trading in foreign currencies . . . and how you can do it too.

DISCLAIMER

The reader should pay special attention to this disclaimer. The purpose of this book is to show how it is possible to make a profit investing in currency. No guarantee or assurance is given, however, that any reader using the indicators, methods, or other materials mentioned in the book will have a successful investment. Every effort has been made to include the most accurate information available; however, the reader should seek out his or her own up-to-the-minute information and not rely on material contained in this book. Readers should consult with their accountant, attorney, or other personal financial advisor before making any investment.

1

There's money to be made in money

AT THE ONSET it is important to understand that when we speak of buying and selling currency, we are not talking about going to a financial supermarket and putting a few baskets of quarters, dimes, and half dollars in our shopping cart. (Although some people who invest in bags of U.S. silver coins dated 1964 and earlier do, in fact, buy exactly in this fashion. We'll discuss this in Chapter 12.)

What we are concerned with is exchanging U.S. dollars into the money of foreign countries (or into gold; see Chapter 11) and then back again into U.S. dollars. Along the way we intend to get more U.S. dollars back out of the exchange than we put in and that represents our profit.

How does one exchange U.S. money for foreign currency? It's really quite simple. Let's say that you're planning a vacation to Germany. In Germany, the currency in use is Deutschemarks (abbreviated DM). If you want to buy a suit, gasoline, or a sandwich, you'll need to pay for these items in

2   Buying and selling currency for profit

Deutschemarks. Therefore, either here in the U.S. before you leave or in Germany once you get there, you'll have to exchange your U.S. dollars for Deutschemarks. Let's say that on the day you make the exchange (here in the U.S. at an exchange counter at the airport) the ratio of DM to U.S. is .5 to 1. What does that mean?

It simply means that it takes more than one Deutschemark to equal the dollar. At .5 to 1 it takes exactly 2 DM to equal one dollar. (Note, the ratio is never constant. It fluctuates and that is the whole basis for making a profit in the field.)

If you feel that you will need $1,000 US for your trip to Germany, you hand this amount over to the currency exchanger and you receive 2,000 Deutschemarks. These you will now have available to spend during your vacation.

Does this mean that you can buy the equivalent of $1,000 U.S. dollars worth of goods and services in Germany with the 2,000 Deutschemarks? Not exactly. The exchange of Deutschemarks into commodities will be close to the amount you could exchange dollars into commodities for here, but it will not be exactly the same. (See Chapter 3.)

Now, let's say you get on your plane in New York and fly directly to Germany. As you arrive at the airport, you realize that you forgot to take your pet beagle to the animal shelter before you left. Instead, she is still in your house. There is no one you can call to handle this for you and, since you are extremely loyal to your dog (not to mention your furniture and rugs), as soon as you can, after landing in Germany, without spending a mark, you get on another plane (using your charge card to pay for the fare) and head back to New York.

You left on Tuesday, but because of waiting in airports and flight time you arrive back on Wednesday. You immediately go to the exchange counter to get U.S. dollars. (Have you ever tried to pay a U.S. cab driver in Deutschemarks?)

You learn that during your brief stay outside the country, the ratio of DM to dollars has changed. Now it's .51 to 1—a change of one cent.

You hand over your 2,000 DM. The exchanger multiplies the DM by .51 (2,000 x .51) and hands you back $1,020. Your brief excursion has netted you a profit of $20 on the exchange rates. Of course, for the service, the currency exchanger extracts a small fee which eats into your profit. Nevertheless, note that the $20 profit was made simply by buying one day at one rate of exchange and selling the very next day at another, higher rate of exchange.

Of course, you may reasonably ask, what's the advantage of making $20? With inflation the way it's been, that's barely enough to cover the cab fare. But, consider, what if instead of $1,000, you had originally exchanged $100,000? Your profit over the same period of time would have been $2,000. If you had exchanged $1 million, you would have made $20,000.

This is not to say, of course, that you need to invest $100,000 or $1 million to make money on the currency exchange. It is possible to do it with far less. The point is that a profit on exchange rates can be made.

How much less investment may be necessary? Consider the case of a friend of mine, Phil, who didn't go to a currency exchanger, but instead bought currency on the futures market.

Phil had traveled to Germany, Switzerland, and other foreign countries and had been impressed by the profit he could make on the exchange rates. He decided to see if he could use the same principle to make much larger profits.

Phil did a little guesswork and determined that the currency of Switzerland, the Swiss franc (abbreviated SF), was too low in its relationship to the U.S. dollar. He figured that in the very near future the Swiss franc would be worth more, in terms of U.S. dollars, than it then was.

Deciding to gamble on his guess, Phil took $5,000 out of the bank. He could have gone to a currency exchanger and simply converted the money into Swiss francs. At the time the exchange rate was about $.53 US. If he had done so he would have received back 9435 SF for his $5,000 US. Then he could have hung onto the money waiting for the price to go up.

Instead, he took the money to a commodities broker with

4 Buying and selling currency for profit

instructions to buy a future contract for Swiss francs. We'll discuss what "futures" are in detail in Chapter 10, but for now, let's not worry about the mechanics of the transaction, but rather how gain or loss can be made in the currency futures market.

Phil learned that with his $5,000 put up as a good faith deposit, he could buy 125,000 Swiss francs to be delivered to him several months in the future. The price of the contact was $.53 per SF. This meant that when the SF were finally delivered to him, he would accept all 125,000 of them, paying $.53 US per franc or $66,250 U.S. dollars. If he accepted delivery of the Swiss francs, he would indeed have to come up with $66,250 U.S. dollars plus broker's commission.

Phil, however, had no intention of accepting delivery of the Swiss francs. He counted on the price going up before his delivery date. At that time he would sell the contract to someone else and pocket the difference between the $.53 he bought for and whatever higher price he sold for.

It turned out that Phil's guesswork was correct. He bought on May 15, 1978, for $.53. By October the price was $.68 and he sold his contract.

What it meant when he sold was that another investor agreed to buy all 125,000 Swiss francs from him at a price of $.68 US per franc. (Why would another investor do this? Because that other person figured the price would go even higher and he could do the same thing Phil had done.) Buying at $.53 US and selling at $.68 meant that Phil made a profit of $.15 on *each* franc. Multiplied by 125,000 Swiss francs, that meant that Phil's investment brought him back $18,750! And he still had the original $5,000 he deposited, less broker's commission (about $75).

Compare this with simply buying Swiss francs at a currency exchange: $5,000 exchanged into Swiss francs at $.53 we saw yielded 9435 Swiss francs. Taking those francs back and trading them for U.S. dollars at $.68 would yield $6,415.80 or a profit of only $1,415.80. It doesn't take much imagination to see that investing in currency futures yields potentially far higher profits than simply exchanging currency for other currency.

Unfortunately, there's also another side to the coin. While profits may be higher, losses may be higher as well . . . and come far more swiftly.

Swings of .15 in the Swiss franc in just a few months are rare (although a swing of .21 did in fact happen between May and October in 1978). But consider for a moment what would have happened if the Swiss franc took a little dip down, before it skyrocketed up. Let's say that Phil bought 125,000 SF at .53 US and a week later the market had moved to .49—a drop of just 4 cents. He bought 125,000 at .53 US or the equivalent of $66,250. If the price dropped to $.49 US, at 125,000 Swiss francs the value would now be $61,250 U.S. dollars. The contract would have lost $5,000 in value. Where would this $5,000 come from? It would have come from Phil's deposit—his margin. A drop of just 4 cents in the value of the Swiss franc before it began skyrocketing in price up 15 cents would have wiped Phil out.

All of which goes to show that in order to be successful (whether you simply exchange currency or play the futures game) in the currency market you must know both *what* and *when* to buy and sell. (Knowledge of how to limit losses and increase gains also helps and this will be covered in Chapter 10.)

Our friend Phil got out of the market just in time, for him. At the end of October of 1978, President Jimmy Carter announced that the U.S. would intervene to support the price of U.S. dollars and the Swiss franc plunged over the next week wiping out much of the gain it had made earlier. If Phil had continued in the market just a few days more, he could have lost not only the profit he made, but his entire investment as well.

What was Phil's secret? How did he know which currency to buy? And when to buy and sell it?

That's what this book is all about. In order to know which currencies are likely to go up in value in relation to the U.S. dollar and when (or, conversely, to know if the dollar is likely to increase in value relative to other currencies), it is necessary to know something about international trade, currency, and economics. Admittedly, this is a tough subject, but one which we'll try to handle with no more difficulty than you've thus far encountered in this chapter.

But first, let's put the endeavor into perspective. A thorough study of the subject requires the reading of a good number of economic texts, the studying of numerous graphs and charts, and the securing of the latest information from a large number of countries. (Check the Appendix for sources for this information.) And even once you have all the information, there is the problem of interpreting it.

As we've seen, there's money to be made (and lost) in currency; economists, politicians, and bankers are always sniffing at the signs, hoping to uncover the critical information that will tell them exactly what's going to happen in the future. Unfortunately, this tends to result in as many opinions as to what causes currency to move up and down in value and when as there are people offering them. About the only consensus I can find is that most experts relate currency values to something called national "health." This would suggest that the appropriate professional to consult for advice would be a medical doctor—that's not very helpful for someone seeking economic information.

Trying to eliminate the experts and going directly to the economic indicators may only magnify the problem. Nearly every expert has his or her own pet indicators.

I've made a list of the different indicators that I've seen people use. Here are some of them:

    Retail Sales
    Personal Income
    Leading Economic Indicators
    Real Spendable Income

Central Bank Reserves
Reserve Assets
Unemployment
Retail Price Index
Wholesale Price Index
Unit Labor Cost Index
Weighted Average Dollar Index
Balance of Trade
Real Spendable Earnings
Budget Deficit
Industrial Production Index
Money Supply
Factory and Durable Goods Orders
Index of Industrial Production

This is only a partial list. It is, however, a complete fog for most individuals. Analyzing and consulting *all* the economic/currency indicators and drawing significant conclusions from the analysis becomes impossible for almost anyone except the experts at the International Monetary Fund and in the international departments of the largest banks. These people spend a lifetime understanding this information; and then, as we've seen over and over again in the past, even they are sometimes wrong.

All of which goes to say that this is a complex subject for which there is no one single, correct answer. I have, however, looked at the indicators. And I have applied them to currency. I have drawn on several which work for me in indicating currency value. For the first half of this book we'll discuss what money is and how these indicators influence it. This all will be in the hope of allowing you, the reader, to learn to use the indicators yourself. (In the last four chapters of the book we'll go into specific investments.)

Will learning these indicators and following them religiously guarantee that you'll be able to make a fortune speculating in foreign currency? Certainly not. If you're old enough to read this book, you're old enough to know that there are no real guarantees in life (except for the proverbial death and taxes). Being successful at currency speculation reminds me of an old friend. He had made a lot of money in currency speculation and before he retired, he said to me, "Making a fortune here is 5% talent and 95% hard work . . . and 100% luck!"

CHART 1A Index of value change in selected foreign currencies relative to the United States dollar Credit: New York Mercantile Exchange

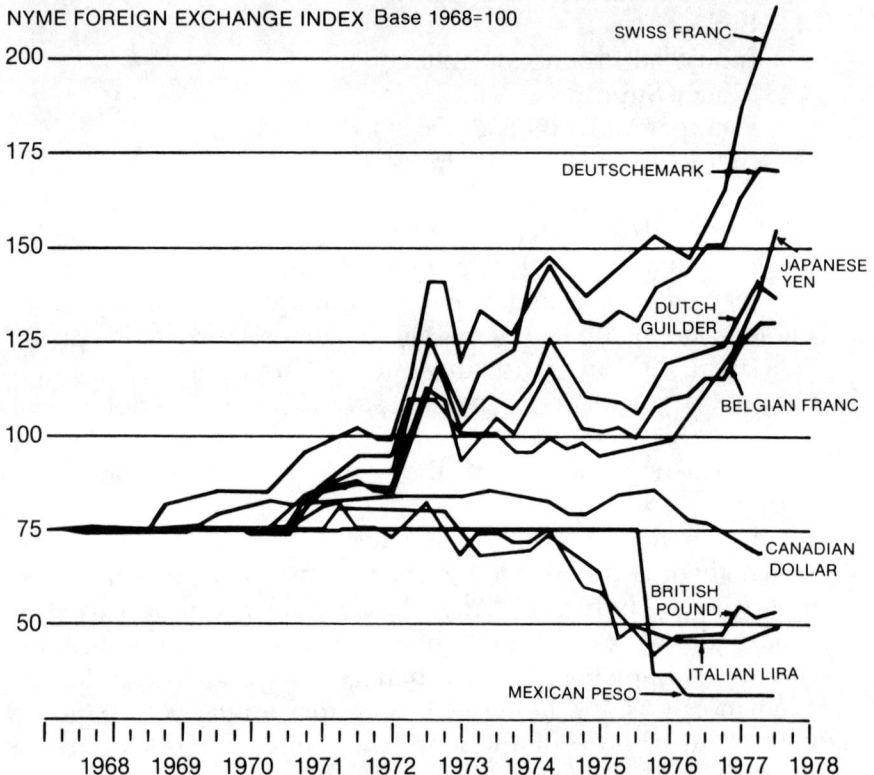

Note to the reader

The next seven chapters will explain the fundamentals of what currency is and what influences currency exchange rates. If this is already familiar material to you, you may skip over to chapters 9–12.

2

Money as a commodity

MONEY ACTS like a commodity in many ways. By this I mean that like cattle, oil, and orange juice, it can be bought and sold and is subject to the "law of supply and demand." In order to gain a working understanding of currency markets, it is essential that the commodity nature of money be understood.

Supply/demand/price—the unwritten law

We'll get to some examples that illustrate how money is used as a commodity within a few moments, but first let's agree on what we mean by the law of supply and demand. This is probably the most quoted phrase in economics, and although most people have a fairly good understanding of what it basically means, few people really understand how it works in detail.

First of all, it really isn't a law at all. It's not written in the

Talmud nor in the U.S. Constitution nor in the civil or criminal code books of any government body. Nor is it a "law of nature." A natural law, such as the law of gravity, might be stated in this fashion. "Any two particles of matter in the universe will attract one another with a force directly in proportion to the product of their masses, inversely in proportion to the square of the distance between them."

This law of nature is immutable and will be the same any time or place in the universe. Not so the law of supply and demand. It may operate 99.99 percent of the time, but not always.

The "law" of supply and demand is just an observation of how people act in a world of scarcity. It tries to make some sense out of the way we all go about getting our desires satisfied. (Note: If this weren't a world where at one time or another almost everything is scarce, there wouldn't be any such law—there wouldn't even be a study of economics because all our desires would be instantly met.)

In reality, the "law" we are speaking of makes more than one observation and it has three parts, not just two. It also takes into account "price." Technically speaking it might more correctly be called the law of supply, demand, and price.

The orange juice demand

It is critical to understand that price is an essential ingredient. Without it we are liable to think that when there is a demand for orange juice, for example, the supply simply tries to rise until it fully meets that demand. We might be led to think that there is a single or static demand. Nothing could be further from the truth. Let's consider the case of orange juice in some detail.

Let us suppose that there is certain demand for orange juice by consumers. They want to drink it with their breakfast cereal in the morning and to add it to their vodka in the evening. But, that demand is not static. Rather, it increases or decreases according to the price of the orange juice. For example, if orange juice costs 35 cents a can, it stands to reason that far more people will consume cans of it than if it costs $35 a can. The demand for orange juice, that quantity of it consumed, depends on the price asked.

The reason that demand varies as we've just illustrated is because of the principle of substitution. At 35 cents a can, a consumer might ask what other commodity he or she might reasonably be able to buy for the same amount of money. It might be a pair of shoelaces, an apple, or half a pack of cigarettes. Given the alternatives, the individual might well figure that it was easily worth spending 35 cents for the orange juice. At $35, however, the choices are far different. Here we might include a complete dinner for two at a good restaurant. Plane fare to visit a friend at a not-too-distant city. A day of fun for several children at Disneyland. At $35 the items that can be substituted for the orange juice are far more desirable; consequently, far fewer people would buy orange juice at that price. In fact, it's probably fair to say that if one million people would buy orange juice at 35 cents a can, probably only a few thousand (and then because of some medical or other pressing need) would buy it at $35 a can.

In fact, we could even estimate the demand for our orange juice in a chart. It might go something like Chart 2A.

CHART 2A Demand for orange juice*

Price	Quantity consumed (in cans)	Price	Quantity consumed (in cans)
.35	1,000,000	5.00	50,000
.50	750,000	10.00	25,000
.75	500,000	15.00	12,000
1.00	350,000	20.00	8,000
2.00	200,000	25.00	5,000
3.00	90,000	30.00	4,000
4.00	60,000	35.00	3,500

*Note: These are not the actual figures for orange juice demand in the U.S. They are simply hypothetical numbers to illustrate the example.

If we were now to plot the demand for orange juice in relation to price, it might look something like Chart 2B.

CHART 2B Demand for orange juice

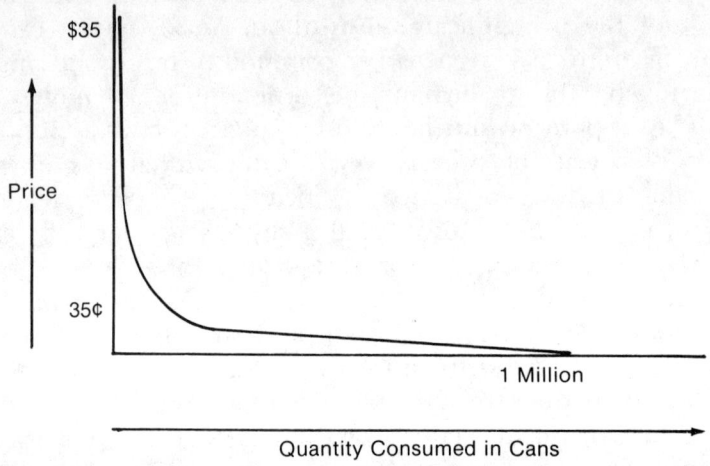

It is critical to understand that we are not talking about different demands. We are talking about a *single demand* for orange juice. When we say there is a demand for a commodity, therefore, what we mean in reality is that there is a *demand curve*—that any given demand cannot usually be expressed as a static point, but can only be expressed in terms of the price. At different prices different quantities are consumed for the same demand. (Note: It does not matter whether we are in a democracy such as the U.S. with an open market or in a socialist state with a controlled economy: Demand is always in terms of substitution; the most convenient expression for substitution just happens to be price.)

There is one exception to this and that comes about when there is a demand regardless of price. For example, if you were dying of a rare disease and there were only one doctor in the world who could cure you, undoubtedly you would demand her services regardless of the price. The demand here would not be limited by the price, only by your ability to pay. There are very few such instances of static demand.

Now that we've seen that demand is in reality a curve on a graph and not a single point, let's consider what a change in demand is. When we say that demand for orange juice is increasing, does that mean we go back to our chart and slide up a few points to a higher price?

No, it doesn't. The demand curve shown on chart 2A is for only a hypothetical demand for orange juice. If there were an increase in the demand for orange juice (brought about, for example, by the flu season when more people wanted to get the vitamin C benefits of the juice and drank more) then we have a whole new demand curve. It might look something like Chart 2C.

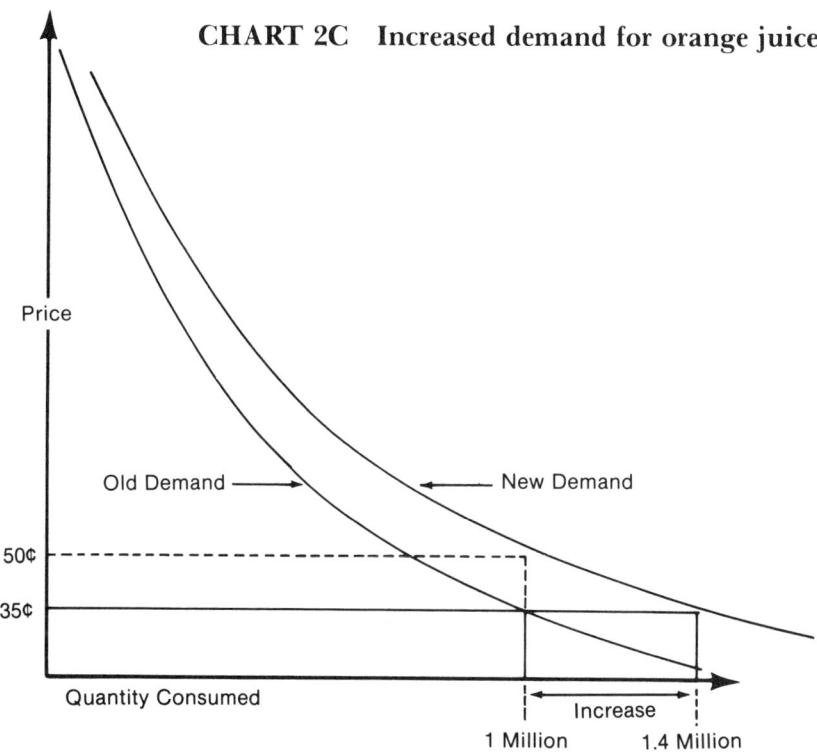

CHART 2C   Increased demand for orange juice

14 Buying and selling currency for profit

Note that on the demand curve there are still multiple levels of consumption based on price. What's different is that at any price, the rate of consumption is higher. And at any rate of consumption, the price is higher. At one million cans, because of increased demand, a price of 50¢ a can may be sustained—an increase of 15¢. At the old price of 35¢, 1.4 million cans may be sold—an increase of .4 million cans. What results from an increased demand is an increased price and consumption for orange juice.

If the 8-ounce can price were 35¢, it might now become 40¢. Or, it might remain at 35¢ or even go down to 30¢. Price also depends on the supply.

Adding the supply

If, at the same time the demand for orange juice increased, producers had anticipated that increase and had also increased the supply, the *price per quantity* would have approximately remained the same. The reason is that there is a similar supply curve to our law (see Chart 2D).

CHART 2D Supply curve for orange juice

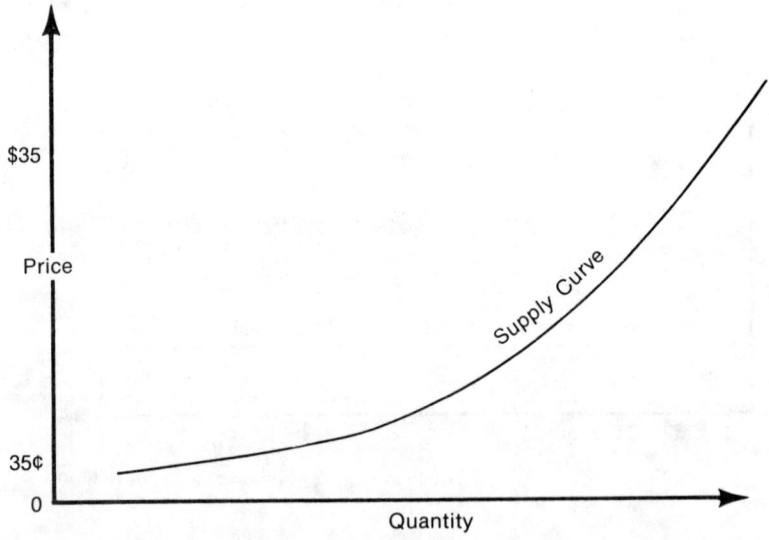

Simply put, the supply of an item available increases as the price goes up. The more people are willing to pay for a commodity, the more there is available. This is frequently seen in the case of gasoline. When gasoline is regulated and the price kept artificially down by government intervention, the amount of the product available at the pumps declines and we may even see lines of cars waiting to fill up. If the price is deregulated and allowed to rise, there is incentive for the producers to get more gasoline to the consumer and the waiting lines disappear.

Sometimes, however, there will be spontaneous increases in supply. This might occur when there is an unusually big harvest of a commodity or when a manufacturer miscalculates and produces too much of a product. Just as in demand, a new increased supply is not expressed along the old supply curve, but creates a new one. Here, at any given price, the quantity is greater than in the old curve. And at any given quantity, the price is lower (see Chart 2E).

CHART 2E Supply curve of increased orange juice supply

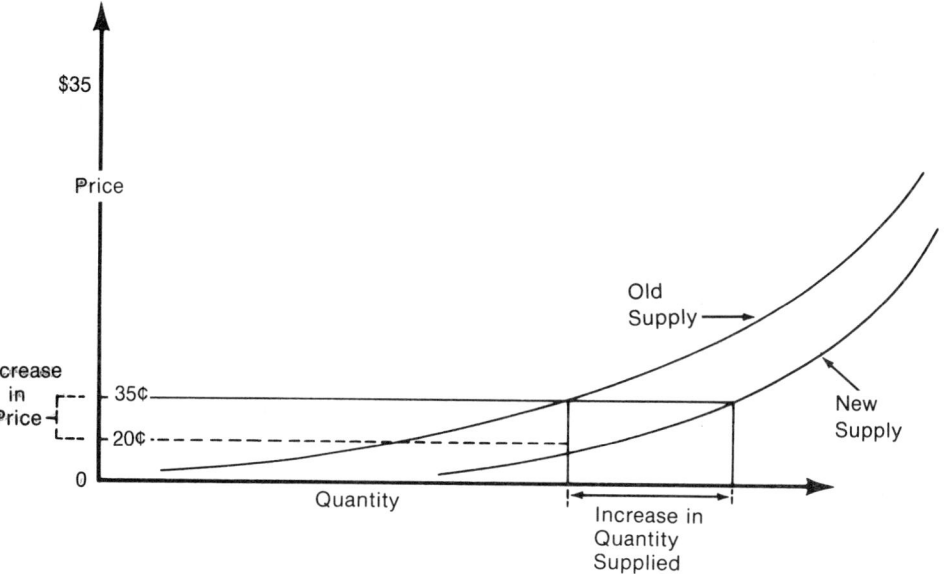

If we now combine what we've learned about supply curves with demand curves, we see that if there is an increase in demand at the same time that there is a corresponding increase in supply, then the price will be roughly about the same (see Chart 2F).

CHART 2F Increase in demand accompanied by increase in supply

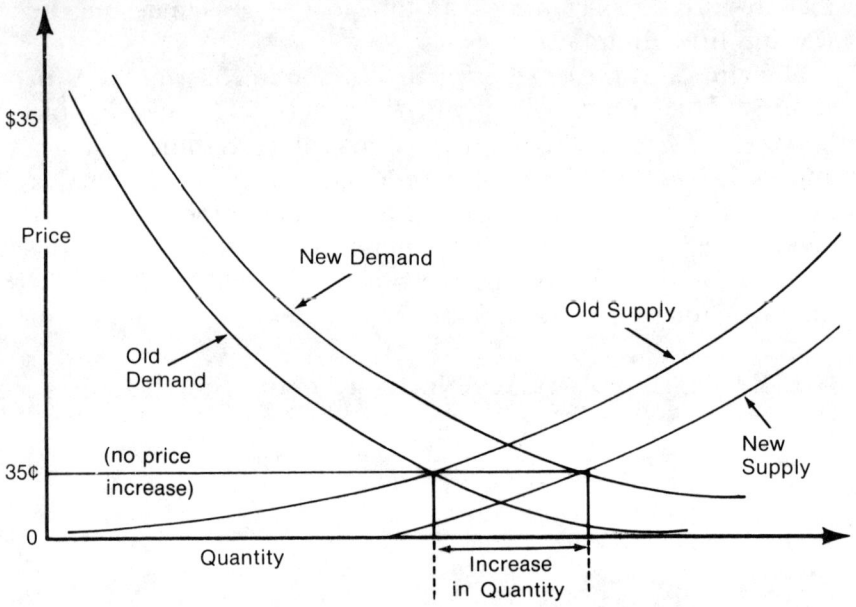

Of course, by all this we should not be led to believe that orange juice or cattle or any other commodity is always offered for sale at an infinite number of prices. Rather, curves such as these are used to determine the optimum price for the supplier, the one which will maximize profit. (Factors such as elasticity of demand, marginal cost of increasing supply and distribution, and marketing also enter the picture. Arriving at a price of 35¢ a can for orange juice is far more complicated than the brief description given here.)

When prices go up

Finally, the critical item we need to get out of all of this is that *if there is an increase in demand without any increase in supply, then prices of a commodity will have to rise* (see Chart 2G).

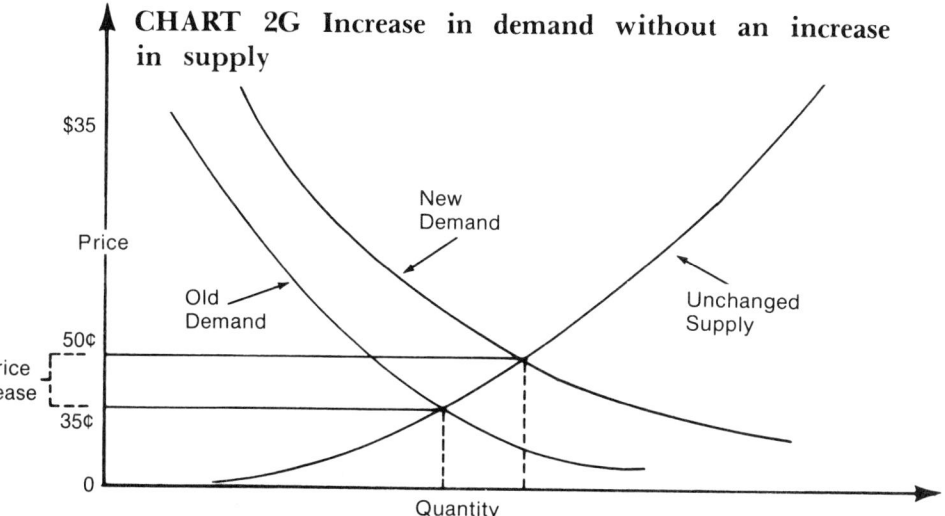

CHART 2G Increase in demand without an increase in supply

As we noted earlier, given the same supply curve, we see that an increase in demand produces both an increase in the amount consumed and an *increase in the amount paid*.

In the short run, however, supply acts differently than demand. While demand may change at the whim of the consumer, supply cannot change so fast. If, for example, there is a sudden and dramatic increase in the demand for beef, the supply will not quickly increase. The reason is that in order to increase beef supply it's necessary to work back down the chain of supply. More cattle will have to be slaughtered; more will have to be fattened; more will have to be bred. It may take a season or even several years to correspondingly increase the supply. What happens in the short run is that there is only so much available. When that's used up, there is no more. In such a situation the demand and supply curves look like Chart 2H.

CHART 2H Short-run effect of an increase in demand without an increase in supply

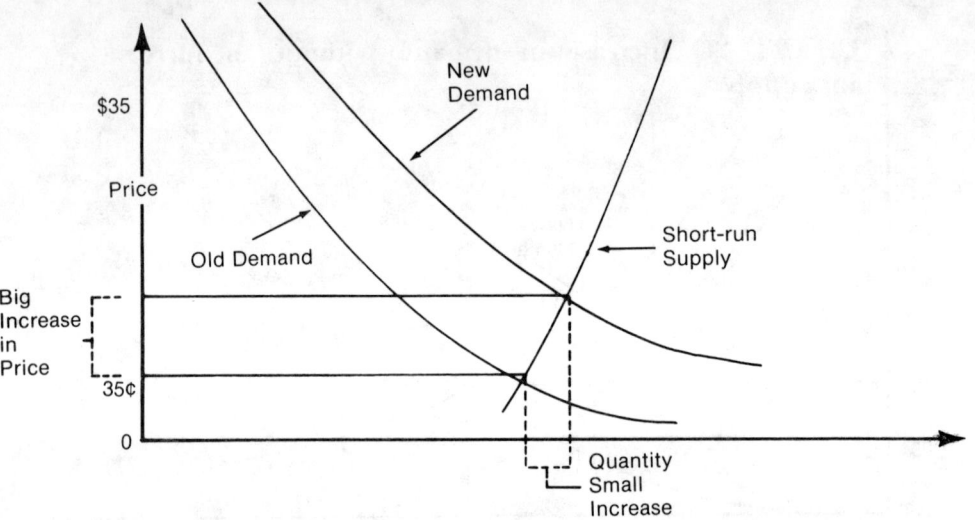

In the short run an increase in demand may increase consumption only slightly (because of limited supply), but increase price drastically. (In practice there is seldom a perfectly static supply; that's why the curve on figure 2H is nearly vertical. As the price rises some products which normally wouldn't be sold are brought onto the market. Growers might offer slightly green oranges or turn out those which had been stored for later in the season. Cattle growers might kill their breeding stock to take advantage of current high prices.)

In review we may say, then, that an increase in demand without an increase in supply acts to dramatically increase prices in the short run. Prices will return to their former level if, eventually, supply is sufficiently increased.*

---

*Manufactured goods act somewhat differently as we'll see in later chapters.

Village money

Now, let's go on and consider money as a commodity.

To do so we'll take the case of a medieval village. In this village there are exactly 20 families. It is an agricultural and primitive manufacturing society, so each family earns a livelihood by either tilling the soil, raising animals, producing goods such as blankets and baskets, or offering a service such as carpentry. Each family produces such things except one whom we'll call the king. The king's sole function is to mint the money that our village uses.

Ours is a fairly sophisticated village. Years earlier when the people first came together, they didn't have money of any kind. Instead they used a barter system. The family that produced wheat would trade some of their wheat to the family that ground the wheat at the mill. The miller would use the wheat to pay the carpenter who fixed the mill. The carpenter would trade work to the blanket-making family for a blanket. The blanket family would trade a blanket to the family that produced chickens and so on. What these villagers discovered, however, was that their barter system really didn't work very well. For example, when the blanket family wanted to purchase a chicken, they agreed that each blanket was worth at least two chickens. But they only wanted (or could only afford) one chicken. One alternative was to cut a blanket in half, but the chicken producer had no use for half a blanket. Therefore in order to buy one chicken, the blanket family had to first go to the wheat-producing family. One blanket was worth a bushel of wheat. They traded for the wheat and then gave the chicken-producing family half a bushel of wheat, kept half for future trading, and received their chicken. Not only was this inconvenient, but it led to problems. For example, when the basket family wanted a chicken (one basket also was worth two chickens) and they went to the wheat family, got their bushel for a basket and came back to the chicken producer to trade half a bushel for a chicken, the chicken producer didn't want to trade. He said he already had enough wheat from the blanket family's trade.

20 Buying and selling currency for profit

The whole problem was solved by one man who owned a gold mine. He mined gold, which really wasn't much good for anything except that it was pretty to look at when made into jewelry. He traded jewelry for the products he needed, at first. But people were so impressed by the shiny metal that he was eventually able to just trade the gold by itself. He shaped it into a convenient round form and put his seal on it. Eventually everyone in the village was willing to accept these little coins in trade and the villagers became very happy. So happy, in fact, that they made him the king.

Things worked out pretty well for the king for a time. He was initially able to produce 200 coins (which averaged out to 10 coins per family) and after that he continued to produce 10 new coins per year. This happened to coincide exactly with the number of coins that were used up each year by villagers who melted them and made jewelry. The supply of coins, therefore, remained constant.

The king, because he originally had the coins, was the wealthiest person in the village, until his mine petered out. Suddenly he could no longer produce coins. At first he thought it was a catastrophe. He had no other source of income. But then he reasoned that, after all, he was the king. If he said something was a coin, it was. So, he made up ten pieces of paper and put his seal on them. He told the villagers they must now accept the paper in exchange for goods and services just as if it were gold. Being peaceable villagers, they all agreed.

The king was delighted. He no longer had to work in the mine. Now he could relax all year long. And one day, while relaxing, he thought to himself, "Why only issue 10 pieces of paper? Paper is cheap. Why not issue 20; then I will be twice as rich?" And he did and the people didn't seem to notice. So the next year he issued 200. And a strange thing happened.

Each villager (with the exception of the king) had roughly the same amount of money. Initially that meant 10 coins per family. When the king issued an additional 10 coins, since there were 20 families, that worked out to about 10½ per family. This made it easier for some families to live, but not a great deal easier. However, when the king issued 200 coins, each family suddenly ended up with roughly twice as many coins as before. They had 10 and received 10 more, and so had 20. They felt much richer.

The basket maker had been paying two coins for a bushel of wheat or 20 percent of his annual income. Now that his annual income had doubled, two coins were only 10 percent. He decided that he could afford to live better, so he bought two bushels instead of the one he had purchased before. The same thing happened to the basket maker. He formerly had bought a chicken with one coin, 10 percent of his income. Now, because he had twice as many coins, he decided to eat more chicken, so he bought two. (Two coins were still only 10 percent of his new income.) This happened throughout the village.

Because of the increase in the number of coins, everyone felt much richer and bought much more. The king had created an entirely new demand curve for all products.

However, there had been no corresponding increase in supplies (no one was making more baskets or blankets, raising more chickens or wheat). And the producers suddenly realized that everyone wanted more of their product. The wheat-producing family saw that the rest of the villagers now didn't mind in the least paying two coins for a bushel, where it had been a struggle before. If they pay two so easily, perhaps they'll pay three, this family reasoned; and so the bushel of wheat was raised to three coins. The same happened for chickens, blankets, and the other items.

Eventually the price rose to four for a bushel. Similarly the price for all the other items and services rose to approximately twice what it had been before. Now, things were about where they had been—doubled income, doubled price. However, in the time that it took for the price to rise, consumption had increased. More wheat, corn, chickens, blankets, and baskets had been consumed than would otherwise have been. Now there was a shortage of supply. And when there is a shortage, the supply curve moves to the left and the price at all levels of supply increases.

Suddenly it took nine coins to purchase a blanket, five for a bushel of wheat, and nine for a basket. Prices had gone up farther than incomes. The people were angry, but they figured to profit from the situation. The basket-making family would make more baskets. The chicken-producing family would raise more chickens, the blanket family more blankets. The carpenter would raise his rates higher. But, now an even stranger thing occurred. The price for reeds for baskets had skyrocketed. So had the price for chicken feed, blanket wool, carpenter's nails, and wood. It was no longer possible to produce commodities and services at the old prices. Because there was more money, the demand (and price) had gone up not for just a single commodity (like blankets or orange juice or cattle) but for *everything!* The people simply couldn't afford to increase their supply curve (thereby bringing down prices) without increasing prices even higher!

The king had created a price inflation. And this made the people very angry.

They forgot that their income had doubled. All they could think of was that wheat which had been two coins a bushel was now five. They would have simply blamed the wheat-producing family, except that the same was true with everything, so they blamed the king. They said that since he controlled the number of coins available, he had to help them out of the inflation. They demanded more coins to pay for the higher prices.

But the king was a wise man (else he never would have gotten to be king) and he had the villagers' best interests at heart. He reasoned that he had caused the price inflation by increasing the supply of coins. More coins meant more demand (both in the number of items bought and the frequency of purchases). Consequently, the answer to the problem was not to give the villagers more coins, but instead to reduce the supply. In answer to his people's demands, our good king announced an immediate tax of 10 coins per family. This would remove the extra coins from circulation and everything would be as it had been before. Needless to say, the king was lynched before the day was out.

Notice two things in particular from this example (we'll refer to other items in it later on). First, money originally started as a commodity. It began as jewelry and then because of its convenience (and relative scarcity) became the standard unit of trade.

Second, money in our example, considered by itself, acted just like any other commodity. When there was an increase in the supply of money, the *money* supply curve moved to the right. The more money available, the more people spent money on products and services. This resulted in higher prices, which is another way of saying the money became less valuable. The more money there was available, the less people wanted (the old amounts of) it. Whereas before two coins were worth one bushel, now it took five coins to buy the same bushel of wheat. People no longer wanted two coins. They wanted one bushel (or five coins).

This is not to say, however, that the money acted the same way at the same time as all the other commodities. It acted exactly opposite in time. As the commodities became more valuable in terms of money, money became less valuable in terms of the commodities.

Therefore, we might reasonably conclude that while money acts as a commodity, it does not act in conjunction with other commodities, but rather in opposition to them.

Finally, in order to facilitate trade between members of the community, a certain money supply was necessary. While an overabundance of money turned out to be bad, a reasonable amount of money was good.

The demand for money

What was a reasonable amount of money? It was when the amount of money allowed for easy consumption of the items produced. In any society those who produce are also those who consume. Individuals produce in order to be able to consume. For example, a laborer works all week to earn $250 in order to be able to buy (consume) $250 worth of commodities. (Of course, the laborer may not intend spending all the money immediately. Some may be saved for future consumption.)

In the most direct sense, although our laborer wants commodities, he doesn't initially express a demand for commodities. Rather, he expresses a demand for money. He doesn't tell his employer to pay him with a pair of shoes, three bags of groceries, and 1/48th of an automobile. He says, "Pay me $250."

Similarly, a supplier doesn't say, "Pay for this pair of shoes by working for me for four and three/fourths hours." He says, "Pay me $35."

There is, therefore, if we gather together all the producers/consumers, an overall need for money. We can express this need in terms of production and consumption (see Chart 2I).

CHART 2I The need for money

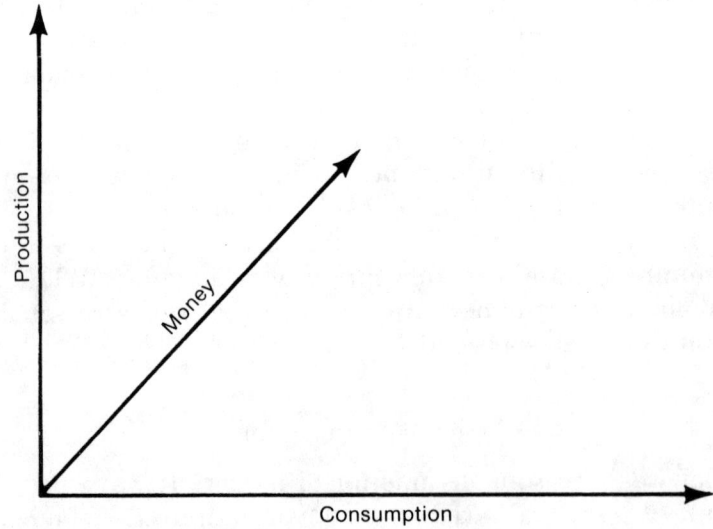

An interesting phenomenon can be observed here. As production and consumption increase, the supply of money should also increase. Is this correct? Let's consider our village.

The original total money supply was 200 coins. That apparently met all needs. Now, let's push our village to the extreme. Let's say that it grew up to be the country of England. Would 200 coins suffice for England today? England requires a much larger supply of money.

Be careful to understand that increasing the money supply to billions of pounds is necessary to facilitate increased commerce. As long as consumption and production of products are in balance, the increase will not be inflationary.

Finally, all other commodites are expressed in terms of price. What is the price of money? In order to understand this we must turn for a moment to borrowing.

The price of money

Borrowing is the spending of future income in the present. For example, if our laborer wants a car that costs $5,000, he may borrow that amount of money from a bank. He will immediately have use of that money, although his present income remains at $250 a week (with a portion committed to paying back the loan). He can borrow/spend the money to buy the car.

When he borrowed, however, he didn't get the money for free. It had a price. Our laborer may have to pay 10 to 12 percent interest per year on his $5,000 just for the privilege of getting it today. Then, he'll have to pay back a certain portion of principal and interest each week (or month) until the car is paid off. Let's say his payment is $160 a month or roughly $40 a week. Our laborer has given up $40 of his present income for whatever number of years (probably four) in order to be able to immediately consume a car. If $10 of that $40 represents interest, then that is the cost of the money to him.

If interest is the cost of money, then how is interest

determined? Part of it is obviously the profit motive of the lender. But, if it were only profit, then everyone could simply keep borrowing as much as they wanted indefinitely. There is another important part.

Our laborer wants to buy more: A new house or a vacation perhaps. Again in order to get the money immediately, he borrows. Eventually, if he borrows enough, he will spend all his present income on payments and interest for future money. He would end up spending $250 a week just on loan payments. In actual practice this never happens. The initial borrowing is quite easy, for lenders can see that the individual can easily both make a loan payment and live on current income. For example, $40 out of $250 is a reasonable amount to pay toward a repayment of a loan. But as more and more of present income is diverted to payment for future cash, less and less income becomes available for new borrowing. Lenders see our laborer as a greater and greater risk. How can he be expected to pay (a lender may ask) $200 a week in loan payments when he only makes $250? What would he live on?

The greater risk would be expressed in terms of higher interest rates. Instead of dealing with a bank at 12 percent interest, he might have to go through a finance company and pay 18 percent. As the risk gets even higher, the only way he can get money might be through a loan shark in which case the interest might be 100 percent or more. From this we can conclude that because the interest rate is an expression, not only of a profit motive in terms of a person lending the money, but also the risk factor of the borrower, *the more borrowed, the higher the rate of interest.*

Now we can plot money as we would any other commodity. One axis is the interest rate, the other is the quantity of money consumed.

As the price (interest rate) of money increases, the quantity borrowed goes down (see Chart 2J).

As the interest rate rises, the quantity available for lending increases (see Chart 2K).

CHART 2J Money demand

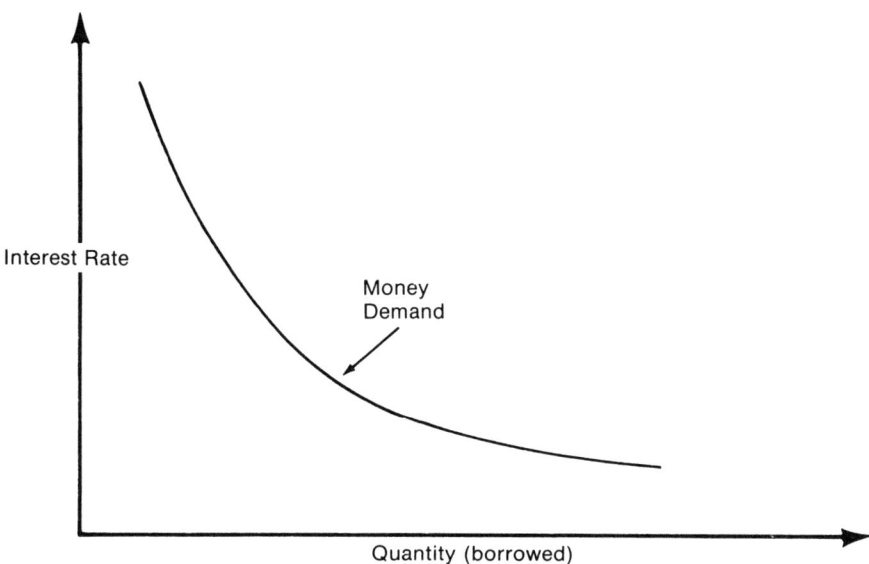

CHART 2K Money supply

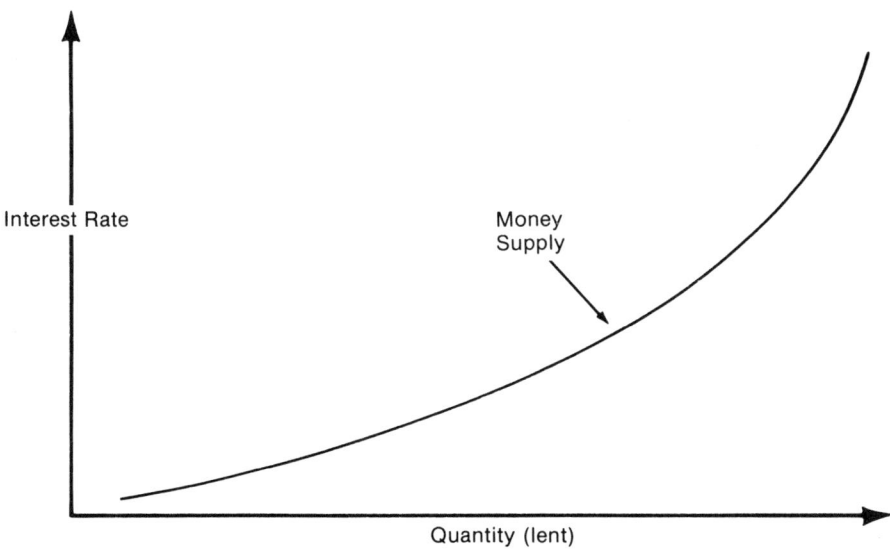

The lower the interest rate, in general, the greater the amount of money borrowed. The higher the interest rate, the less borrowed. (In reality high interest rates are usually caused by a high demand and a decrease in supply of money or by inflation. See Chapter 4.)

Money acts like a commodity. As we've seen, it can be bought and sold, paid for with interest. It also has a direct though opposite relationship to other non-monetary commodities. The more the non-monetary commodities are valued, the less the value of money and vice versa. Finally, increasing the money supply ultimately can decrease the value of money. Now, let's see how this applies to currency exchanging.

3

Productivity—how it determines money's value

WHETHER YOU WANT to buy a loaf of bread, a sweater, or an automobile, if you have the money and can find the product you want, the transaction normally is fairly simple. You give the seller the money and you take the product.

When buyer and seller are in different countries, however, any transaction is far more complicated. It is complicated because each country uses its own currency. When an American wants to buy a Japanese car, he wants to pay for it in dollars. But the Japanese manufacturer wants to be paid in yen. How is the problem solved?

The process of handling foreign trade can be fairly complex, but somewhere in the transaction there has to be an exchange of dollars for yen. The question is, how many yen to the dollar (or the other way around) must be exchanged so that both the buyer and the seller of the automobile are receiving the same value, although in different currencies?

The answer is the exchange rate. If the current rate happens to be 200 yen to the dollar and the car is valued at 800,000 yen in Japan, then the transaction is fairly simple (in terms of currency exchange). The American simply translates the current exchange rate into dollars (800,000 ÷ 200 = $4,000), and discovers that it will cost him $4,000 to "buy" 800,000 yen. He buys the yen, pays the Japanese manufacturer for the car, and accepts delivery.

(In our example we have overlooked numerous other items such as cost of delivery, cost of exchanging currency, and time lag between purchase and delivery. All these also influence the price that will be paid.)

If there were always a constant never changing and fixed rate of exchange no more would need be said about this transaction. (Indeed, there would be no need for this book!) However, the exchange rate, as we've noted, fluctuates widely. While the rate may be 200 yen to the dollar one week, it could be 195 to the dollar the next and 205 to the dollar the following week. That makes a big difference to the buyer and seller. At 195 to one (dollar), 800,000 yen equals $4,103. At 205 to one (dollar), 800,000 yen equals $3,902. Depending on the week of purchase the difference could mean over $200 difference to the American purchaser. Naturally the American purchaser would prefer to pay for the car when the price was cheaper in terms of dollars. The Japanese manufacturer would prefer to sell when yen were worth more.

But, why is there that fluctuation in the exchange rate? If, as we just said, the purpose of the rate is to establish similar values in each country, surely the rate should remain stable over a fairly long period of time. The value of an automobile in the U.S. and in Japan doesn't vary as much as $200 (more or less) every few weeks. Why should the exchange rate vary as much as that?

The easiest way to understand exchange rate fluctuation is to consider how currency exchanges might have begun originally. Let's suppose that we have two countries totally independent of one another, such as Japan and the United States were in the eighteenth century. For this example, however, we'll call our countries red and blue.

Red country and blue country

One day a trader from country red appears on the shore of country blue. He has products of country red to offer. These include ceramic beads, cans of oil, and guns. The people in country blue are very much impressed with what the trader has. However, in order to obtain his goods, they must find something he wants. It turns out they have transistor radios, cameras, and sandals, which the trader much admires. They immediately sit down and begin bartering. How many cans of oil will it take to buy one radio? How many sandals to get one gun? And so forth.

How does the trader from country red determine what he is willing to give in exchange? How do the people of country blue determine what they are willing to give in exchange? The answer is one that we noted in Chapter 2—substitution. The trader from country red has a gun and he wants sandals. How does he determine how many sandals to get for his gun?

Since he is a trader, the determination for him is fairly simple. He knows what he paid for the gun back in his own country. We'll say he paid 20 red dollars. Now he must guess how much he can sell the sandals for back in country red. Our trader is very shrewd, else he wouldn't last in the business. If he estimates that he can sell them for $5 a pair, then he must get at least four pair in order to break even. He needs five pair in order to make a profit (5 pair at $5 red yield $25 red—he only paid $20 red for the gun).

The trader offers the blue people one gun for five pairs of sandals. Now the ball is in the blue people's court. They consider the gun. They've never seen anything like it. They are sure that it is valuable, but just how valuable? They begin thinking to themselves that if they had to sell the gun to some of their countrymen, just how many blue dollars could they

32 Buying and selling currency for profit

get for the gun? They estimate they could get 100 blue dollars for the gun. They already know how much a pair of sandals costs in their country, 15 blue dollars a pair. The trader only wants five pairs or 75 blue dollars worth. By making the trade they can earn a profit of 25 blue dollars. The bargain is made.

In this simple example not only was a gun exchanged for shoes, but a primitive exchange rate for guns was established—100 blue dollars is equal to 20 red dollars, 5 to 1. Does this now mean the blue dollars and red dollars can be used instead of this bartering system (which as we saw in Chapter 2 is very inefficient)?

Not quite. One exchange with both parties not fully knowing the value of the products on the domestic market does not make for setting up a currency exchange ratio. If after a time, however, hundreds and thousands of traders begin going between countries red and blue, they will soon get to know what the values of commodities are in both countries. Profit margins due to lack of information will disappear and will be replaced by something called productivity.

Let's suppose that after some years of trading, country red and country blue are both making guns and sandals. In country blue, however, because they haven't long experience in making guns, they have few trained workers in the field. Also because materials with which to make guns are not readily available here, they must pay high prices for them. And because they have not made guns before, it costs them a great deal to set up manufacturing plants. These new guns produced in country blue are quite expensive. They cost 80 blue dollars to make. However, because country blue has skilled shoe workers, readily available material, and already built plants, they can produce shoes more efficiently at a cost, as we've seen, of 15 blue dollars a pair.

In country red, where our first trader came from, the opposite situation exists. Guns can be produced for 20 red dollars. But sandals, because of unskilled work crews, expensive material costs, and the high price of setting up production, cost five red dollars a pair to make.

Each country, of course, could continue to make its own guns and shoes; however, there's profit to be made for both. By selling a red gun in country blue, the red merchant can get 80 blue dollars, the going price—by selling two, 160 blue dollars. With this money he can buy ten pairs of sandals (and still have five blue dollars left over). Taking the ten pairs of blue sandals back to country red he can sell them for five red dollars apiece (the going rate) or $50, making back all the money he spent buying the guns ($20 apiece or $40) plus 10 red dollars profit.

Of course, the traders from country blue could go to red and do the same thing. They could also sell at a profit for less than the going domestic rate, thereby increasing sales.

In an open market (no government or commercial restraints), with all parties having complete knowledge, it is the productivity or efficiency of people that determines the relative value of commodities. Now a currency exchange ratio can be established. Of course, all trades for all commodities would have to be taken into account, but assuming that they were the same ratio as guns to sandals, the exchange rate would be a compromise, perhaps 3.5 to 1. Once this exchange rate was established, then traders from either country blue or red would be willing to accept the other currency as well as their own.

Of course, productivity changes. Blue country may learn to make guns cheaper; red country may learn to make sandals more efficiently. As these changes occur, overall, traders may become unwilling to accept the old rates of exchange and new rates would have to be established. Over the long-term, this would mean that there would be some fluctuation in the exchange rate.

This all may sound nice enough, but does it really apply? How is productivity tied to the currency rates of real countries?

Efficiency

As we noted, productivity or the efficiency of one country

over another determines the basic trade relationship. If one country could make all items more efficiently than another, then that country would be able to export to all other countries and would need to import nothing. It could select whatever it wanted to receive in exchange for its exports—gold, diamonds, women, men. Fortunately, in industrialized countries that is not the case. (Although it is sometimes the case in terms of countries that have a monopoly on natural resources, such as the Organization of Petroleum Producing Countries [OPEC]. See Chapter 6.)

If we can determine which countries are more efficient, then we have a basis for determining which countries' currencies are going to be more valuable. Of course, we must keep in mind that changes in the rate of efficiency do not happen overnight. Consequently what we shall be looking for here are long-term insights.

The efficiency of a country is not easily determined. For example, when you cross a border there isn't a large sign indicating, "Germany, population 60 million, efficiency index 122.4." We can, however, interpret efficiency in a number of ways. The method I've chosen is to compare industrial output with industrial labor required for that output. Put simply, this means how many hours or how many laborers it takes to produce a product. Since most of the countries whose currency has the potential to be speculated in are industrial nations, picking industrial productivity seemed most appropriate.

Chart 3A indicates the productivity (ratio of total real production to the number of hours worked by all persons) of the U.S. worker (nonfarm). Note that while productivity has risen, it has not risen much since 1967, and since 1975 it has barely risen at all.

By itself, this chart indicates that the U.S., while not losing ground to efficiency, is not getting any more efficient. However, the U.S. productivity can only be meaningful when compared to productivity for other countries. I've chosen Germany, France, Switzerland, England, Canada, and Japan for comparison (see charts 3B-3H).

Productivity—how it determines money's value 35

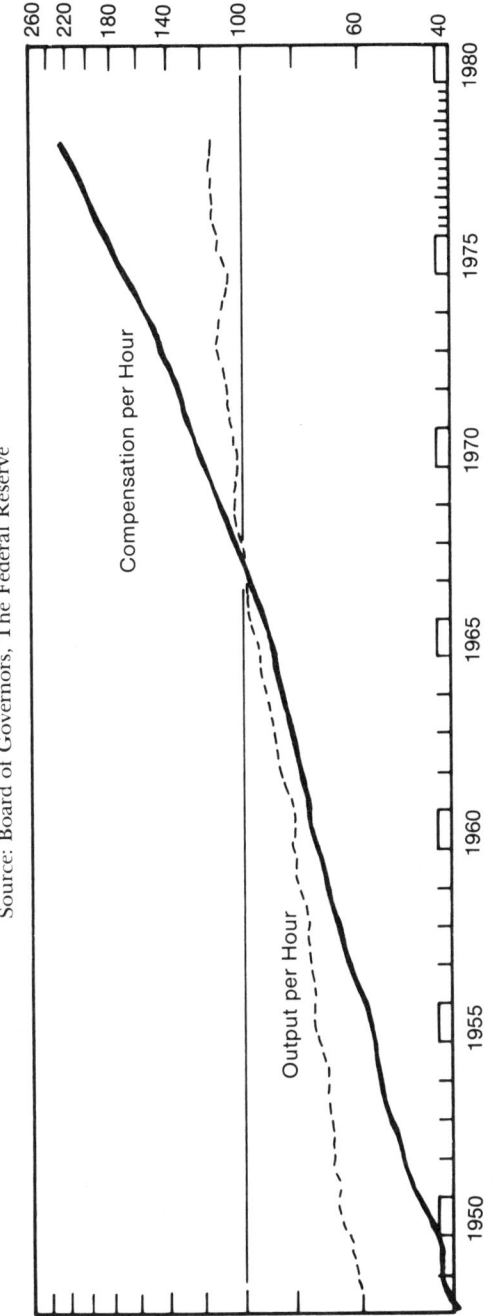

CHART 3A Productivity of American workers
Source: Board of Governors, The Federal Reserve

CHARTS 3B-3H Estimated change in productivity of each country between 1975 and 1978—index*

CHART 3B Germany
1975=0

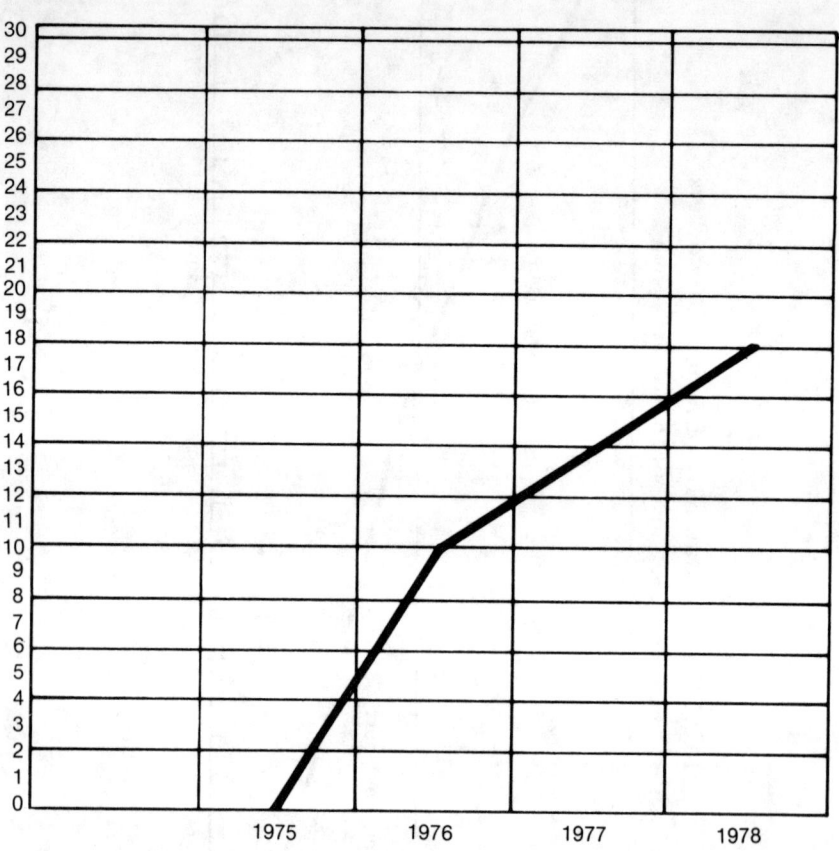

*On charts 3B-3H special attention should be paid to the *direction* and *rate* of change, not the specific amount of change

Source of charts 3B-3H: International Financial Statistics, International Monetary Fund, Nov., 1978

Productivity—how it determines money's value 37

CHART 3C France
1975=0

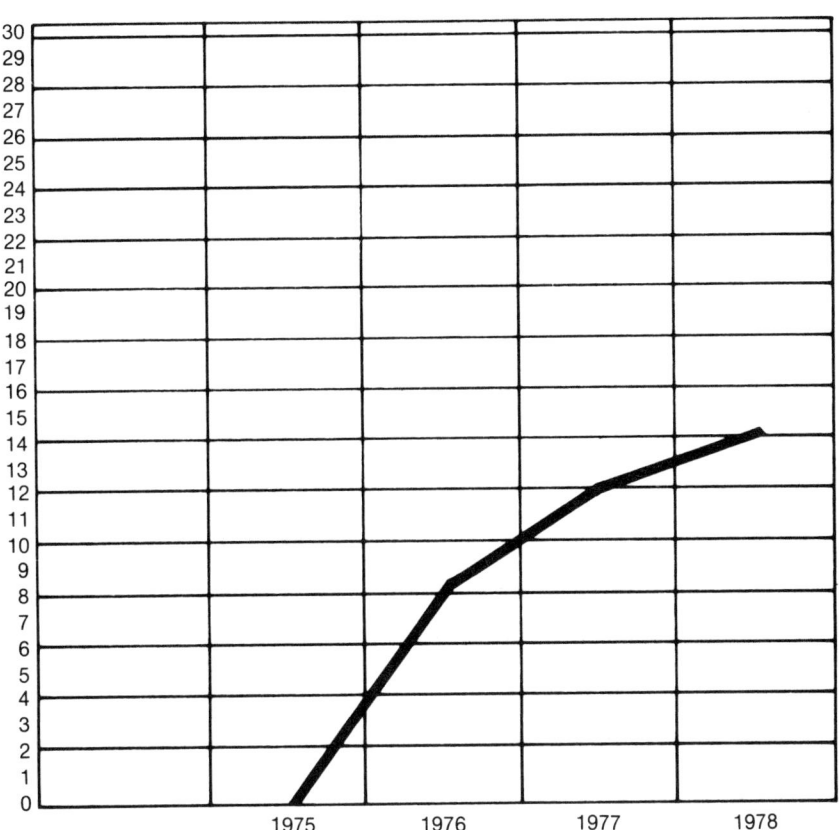

CHART 3D Switzerland
1975=0

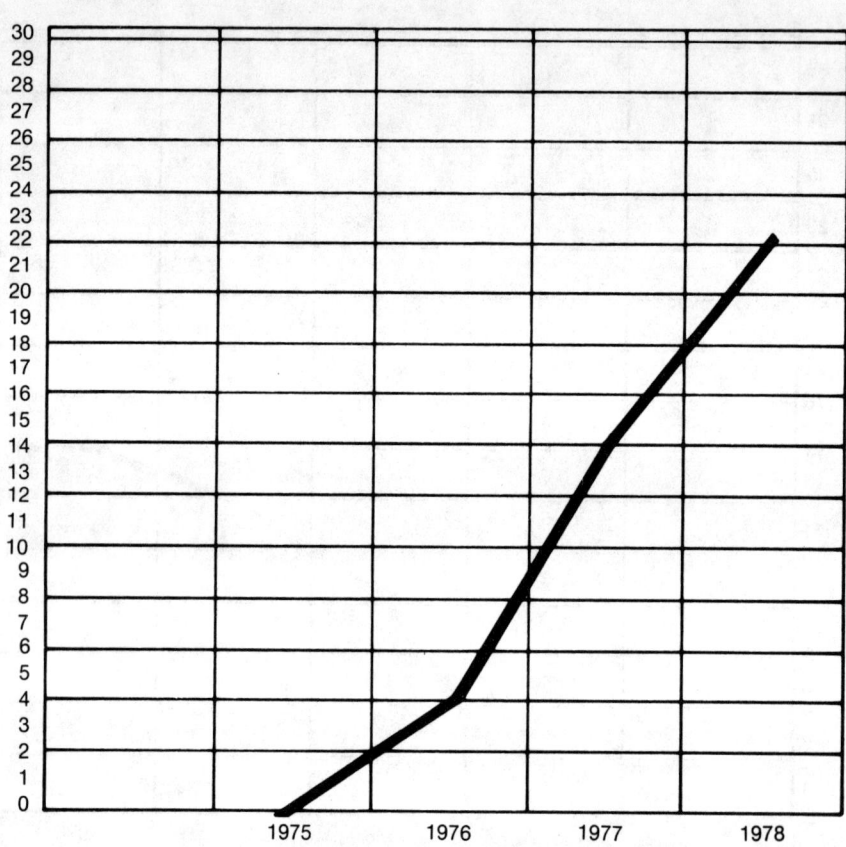

Productivity—how it determines money's value 39

CHART 3E Great Britain
1975=0

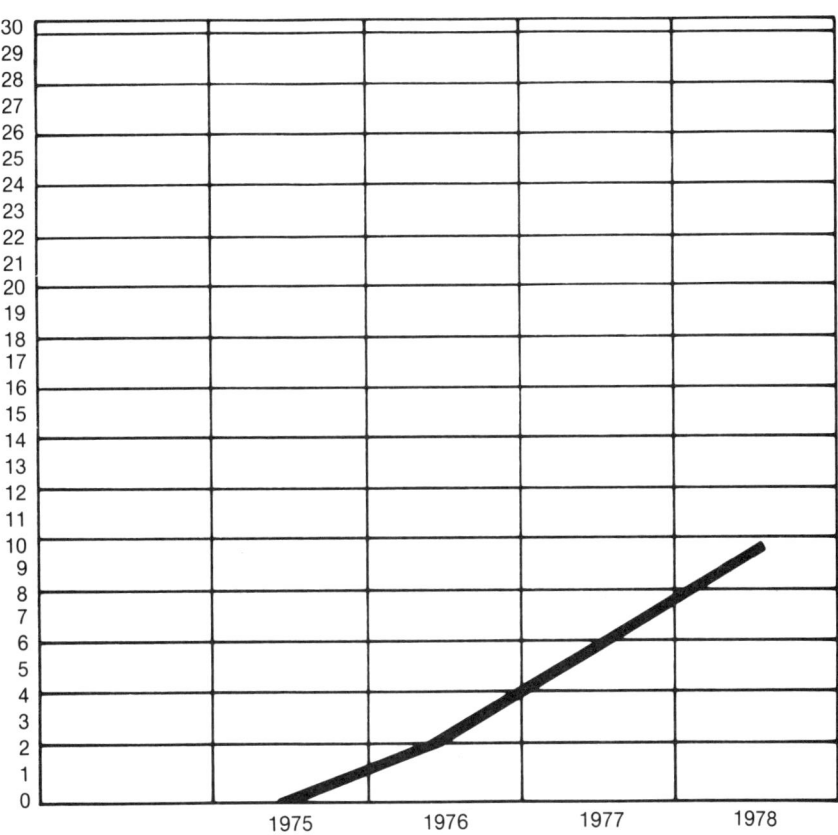

40 Buying and selling currency for profit

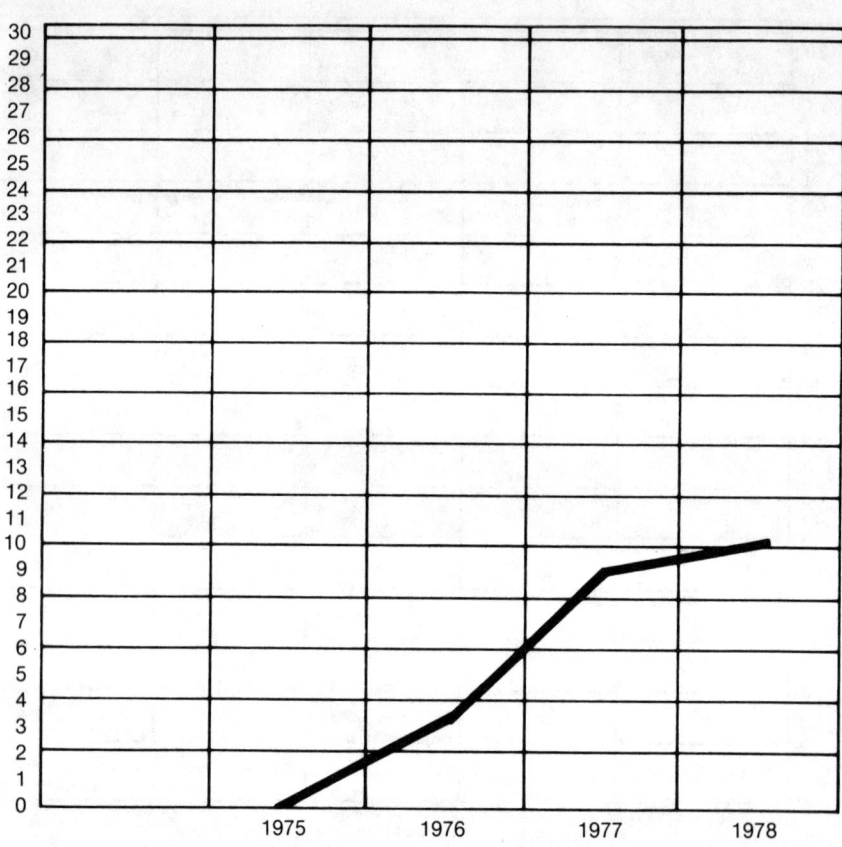

CHART 3F   Canada
1975=0

Productivity—how it determines money's value 41

CHART 3G Japan
1975=0

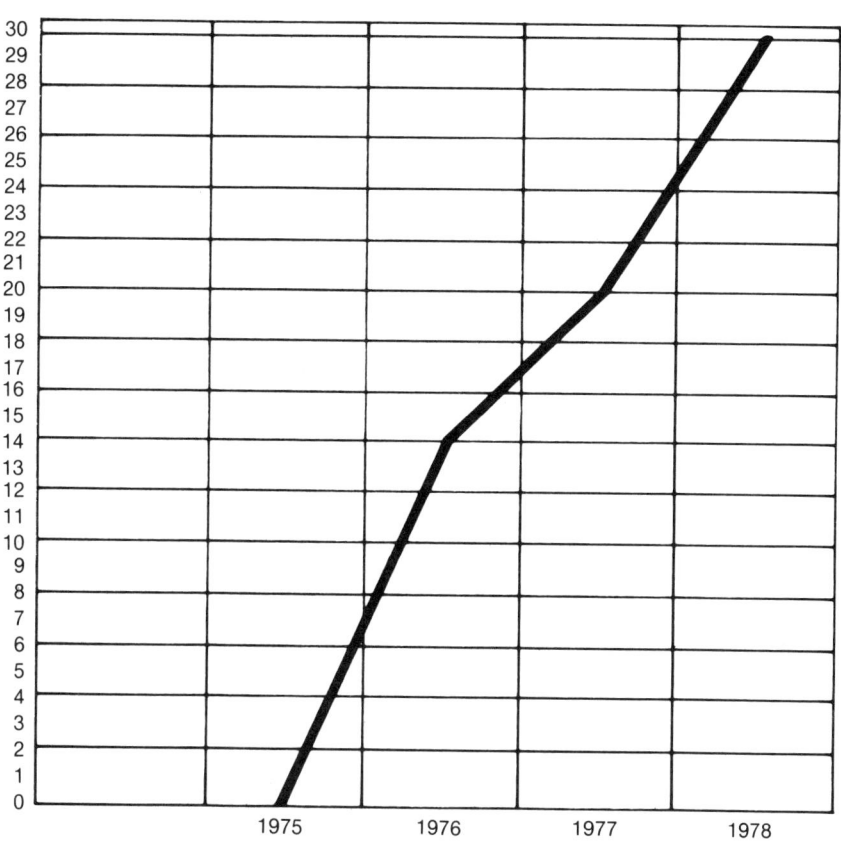

CHART 3H United States
1975=0

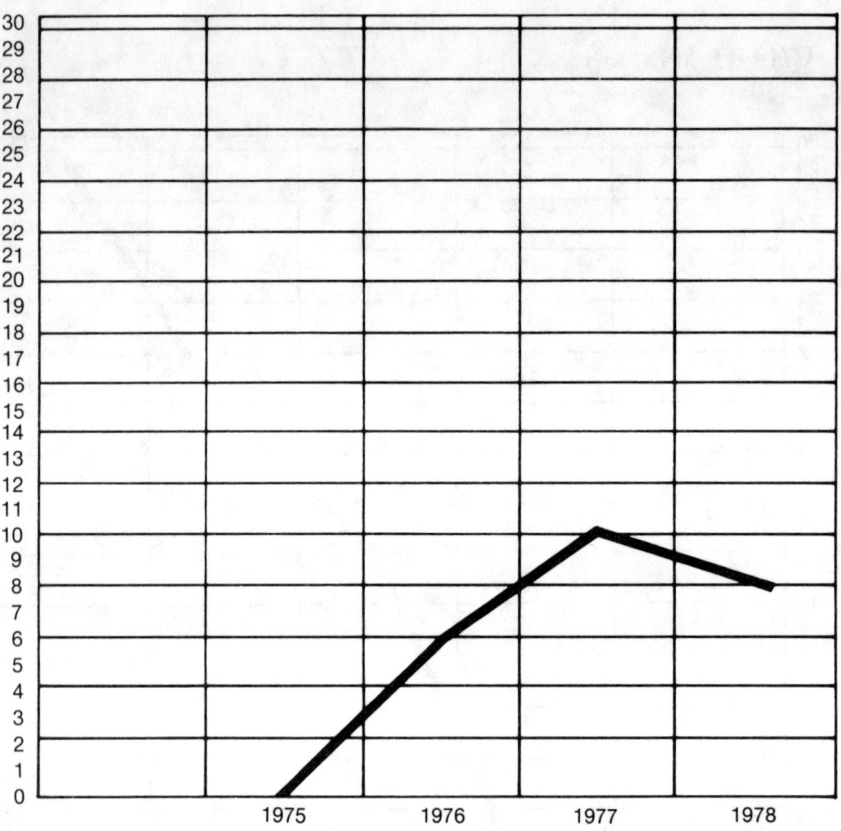

Note: While information for the U.S is readily available, it is more difficult to come by for foreign governments. The sources for charts 3B-3H were the U.S. Federal Reserve Bank and the International Monetary Fund. See Appendix for information on how you can obtain this information directly for yourself.

While Chart 3A indicates numbers of hours divided into products, charts 3B-3H indicate number of workers divided into products. This difference is necessary in order to provide uniform information for different countries.

Note that the chart for the U.S. was the only one to show a drop in productivity in 1978. This might be accounted for by President Jimmy Carter's determination to increase employment. The calculation of these charts divides employment into production. More workers, more hours, and stagnant production could cause a drop in productivity.

Note also that the productivity of the other countries rose, but by different rates. Japan rose the most with Germany and Switzerland following close behind. This rise in productivity becomes much more significant when we compare the value of the currencies of these countries to the productivity charts (see charts 3I-3O).

CHARTS 3I-3N Foreign currency value for each country based on spot exchange rates—index
Solid lines = dollar prices
Dotted lines = weighted average prices
March 1973 = 100
Source of charts 3I-3N: Board of Governors of the Federal Reserve

CHART I German mark

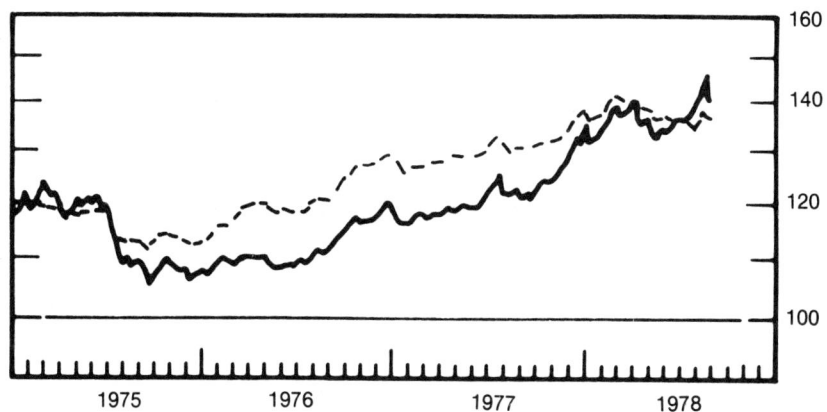

CHART 3J   French franc

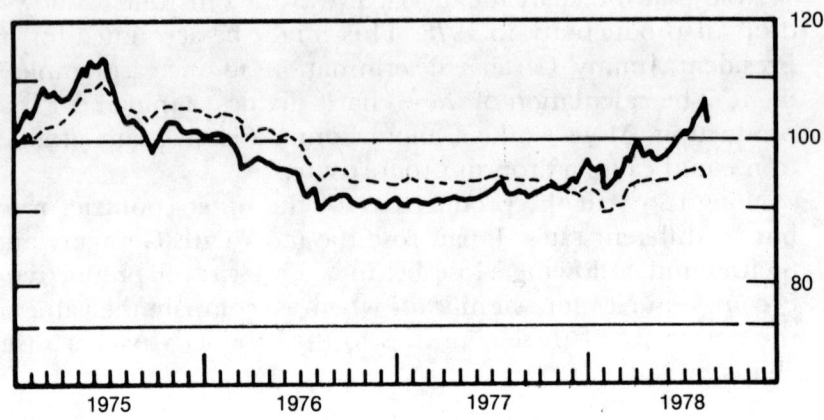

CHART 3K   Swiss franc

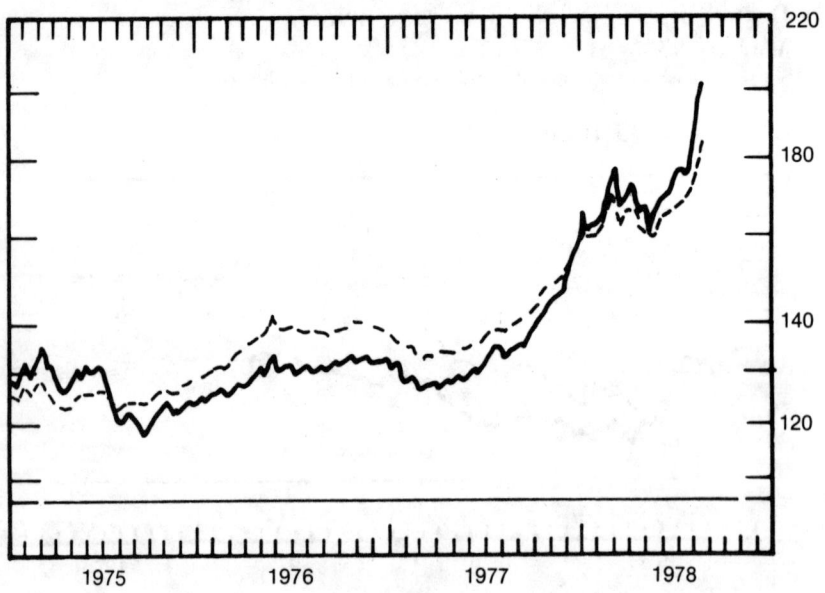

CHART 3L United Kingdom pound

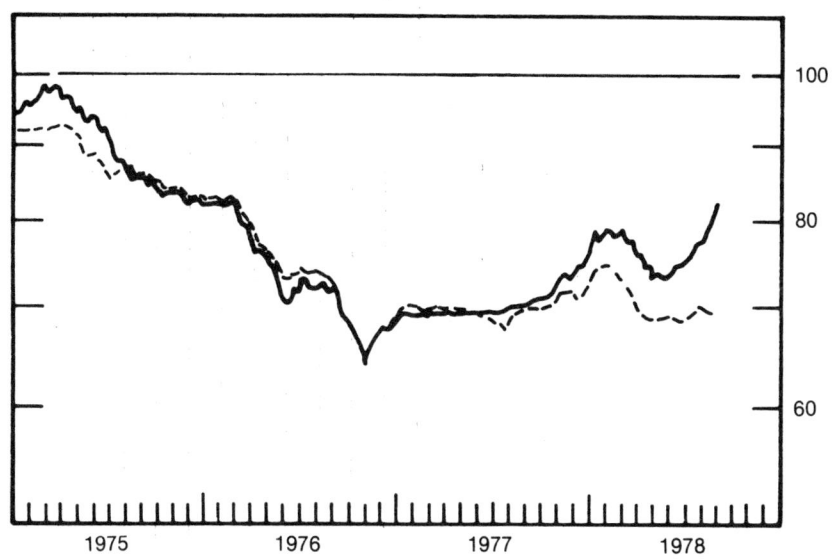

CHART 3M Canadian dollar

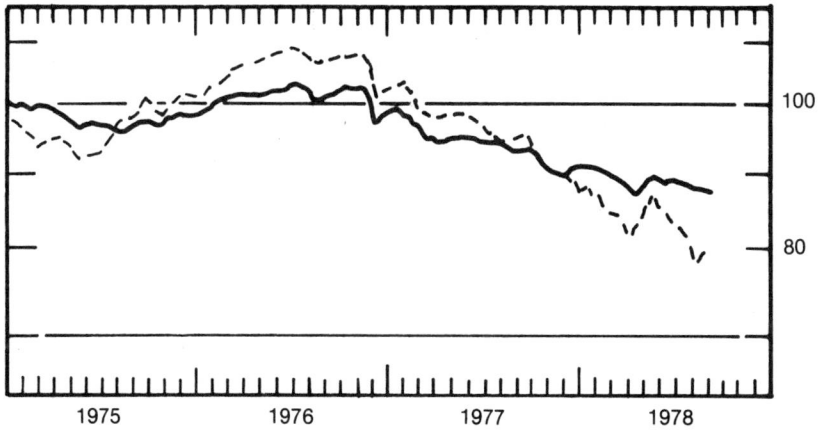

CHART 3N Japanese yen

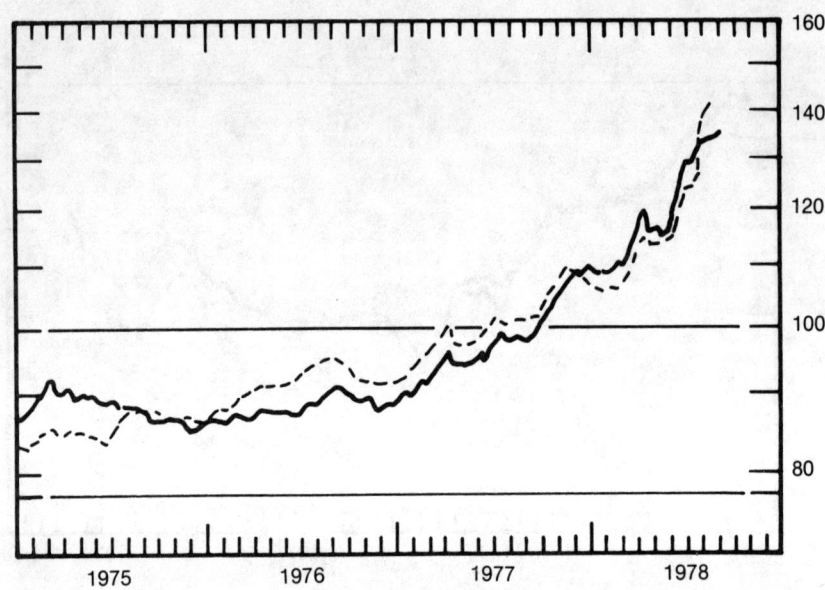

CHART 3O Foreign currency price of United States dollar
Dotted line = weighted average prices
March 1973 = 100

RATIO SCALE, MARCH 1973=100

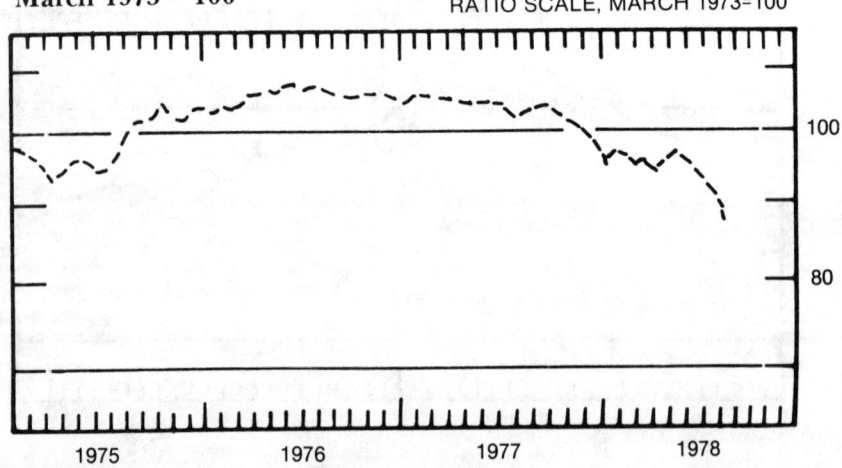

Source: Board of Governors of the Federal Reserve

It is not too difficult to see that *in general* the currency values have followed the productivity curves. Those with steep upward productivity curves such as Japan and Switzerland have seen their currency rise in value relative to the dollar. Germany with a moderate upward productivity curve has seen its currency go up moderately, relative to the dollar. While those with only modest productivity increases, Canada, England, and France, have seen their currencies remain relatively constant or drop in value relative to the dollar. Which is to say what we've suspected all along, currency of countries with high productivity rates is worth more than currency of countries with low rates.

Of course, the trends of the currencies have not been mirror images of the productivity of countries. Rather, the lines have the same general direction. But in some cases there are aberrations, such as the drop in value of Canada's dollar relative to the U.S. dollar.

From this we can reasonably conclude that if in the next few years currency continues to follow productivity as these charts indicate it has in the past, by watching productivity of various countries, by comparing it, we can get a rough long-term view of what currency is going to do.

It would be much more helpful, of course, if we could get a closer, more short-term view of what's likely to happen in the future. In order to do that, we must take into account another influence on currency—inflation.

4

Inflation—and how it affects currency rates

INFLATION is a loss in value of money. If, however, you were to go to the library and try to look up inflation rate directly in almost any source book, you would be disappointed. Inflation is simply not listed as such. Because it involves a loss of money value, it is expressed as an increase in price for commodities. In the library you would be referred to a number of sources, including the Consumer Price Index and the Wholesale Price Index.

Consumer Price Index

These indices measure the increase in price of a great variety of products and thus, indirectly, measure the loss of value in the dollar. For example, if the price index goes up 10 percent a year, that, in effect, means that the value of the dollar has gone down 10 percent a year. Note, the exact numbers used in the index are seldom of interest. What matters is the percentage change from year to year (or month to month).

Some have argued that when discussing world currency, it is best to use the Wholesale Price Index (WPI). The argument usually goes that the WPI more closely reflects those products which are actually traded on world markets than does the Consumer Price Index (CPI) which includes a number of goods and services that are strictly domestic in nature. This argument is a good one; however, the Consumer Price Index tends to affect interest rates at home, and since interest rates are critical to an understanding of currency, my feeling is that it is best to stick with the CPI, which I shall do for the remainder of this book. (Note: For purists, the following information can be interpolated for the WPI by simply substituting its figures for CPI figures and recalculating the results.)

Inflation and currency

In order to understand how inflation affects currency rates between different countries, let's go back to our example of the medieval village. When the king issued paper instead of gold coins, he debased the currency—he made it less valuable in the village.

This debasement would make it extremely hard for our villagers to trade with towns that had different money. People in town who saw that prices in the village had doubled would not want to accept the villagers' paper money, at least not on the same terms as before. If prices doubled, then the money was worth only half as much. The towns would only accept the paper money if they received twice as much. A new exchange ratio would be established.

Price inflation, therefore, in addition to productivity, helps determine exchange rates.

In earlier centuries the problem of inflation (or loss in value of currency) was handled differently than it is today. Rather than having an exchange rate between currencies of the world, there was at times a single currency used by many countries. A few hundred years ago it was the Spanish dollar. (At one time it was the Greek tetradrachm.)

Used extensively in the Americas, the Spanish dollar was made of a standard value of silver and, since all countries considered silver valuable, it was readily accepted in exchange for commodities in a dozen different lands.

Trade dollars

Few Americans are aware that in 1873 in order to facilitate trade between the United States and the Orient, the U.S. government issued its own "trade dollars." These coins contained 420 grains of silver compared to 412½ grains for domestic dollars. They were to be used exclusively by merchants and were not for circulation here in this country. They were intended to become another Spanish dollar. (The trade dollar was not particularly successful. Although tens of millions were minted, the habit of Chinese merchants of taking a small portion or "chop" out of the dollar to test for silver content, made them undesirable for trade. Five years later in 1878 mass production was halted, although the series did not officially end until 1885.)

Modern countries, however, because of the massive volume of exchanges and the high prices involved, cannot do business in coins. They must use paper or "fiat" money. Yet, how to make paper money as universally accepted as silver coins once were?

Golden money

The answer was to tie the money to gold. At one time foreigners could redeem all U.S. paper money for gold at the fixed rate of $35 to an ounce of gold. Since gold was valued in all countries, the U.S. dollar became, particularly after World War II, a universal currency, much more so than even the Spanish dollar had become. In the early 1970s, however (for reasons we'll see in Chapter 5 on balance of payments), the U.S. stopped redeeming its currency with gold.

But, it may reasonably be asked, if the dollar is not pegged to gold, then why do other countries accept it? What establishes its value? The answer is that its value was established originally, as we saw earlier, by productivity, not by gold. Gold was only a safety valve to protect against debasement. Its value today, put most simply, is the original value established relative to productivity, stabilized by the gold standard, *plus any increase in productivity* relative to other countries, *minus any inflation*. (We'll see later that trade and interest rates are also important considerations.)

What this means in regard to inflation, then, is that if the U.S. has a high inflation rate and another country has none, our currency will be worth less against the other country's currency.

The result is that a country with inflation will find its currency worth less in comparison to a country with no inflation. In the modern world, almost all countries have inflation. The result is that the country with the least inflation has the most valued currency and vice versa.

Comparing inflation rates

Charts 4A-4H show the inflation rates since 1970 between several countries we've been considering. Probably the most notable thing about these charts is the enormous swings upward in 1974 and 1979. Few would dispute that this was caused in part by the great increase in oil prices instituted by the OPEC nations. Not only did the price of oil and oil products such as heating oil and gasoline go up, but all oil-related products (which in our modern society involves many items) also shot up. After that first dramatic increase, inflation dropped in all countries, but not to the same levels. By 1978 it dropped almost to zero in Switzerland and was also very low in Japan and Germany. England was about the same level as

CHARTS 4A-4H Rate of inflation in each country (measured by the Consumer Price Index—percent of change from corresponding period of prior year) Source of charts 4A-4H: International Financial Statistics, March, 1980, International Monetary Fund.

CHART 4A Germany

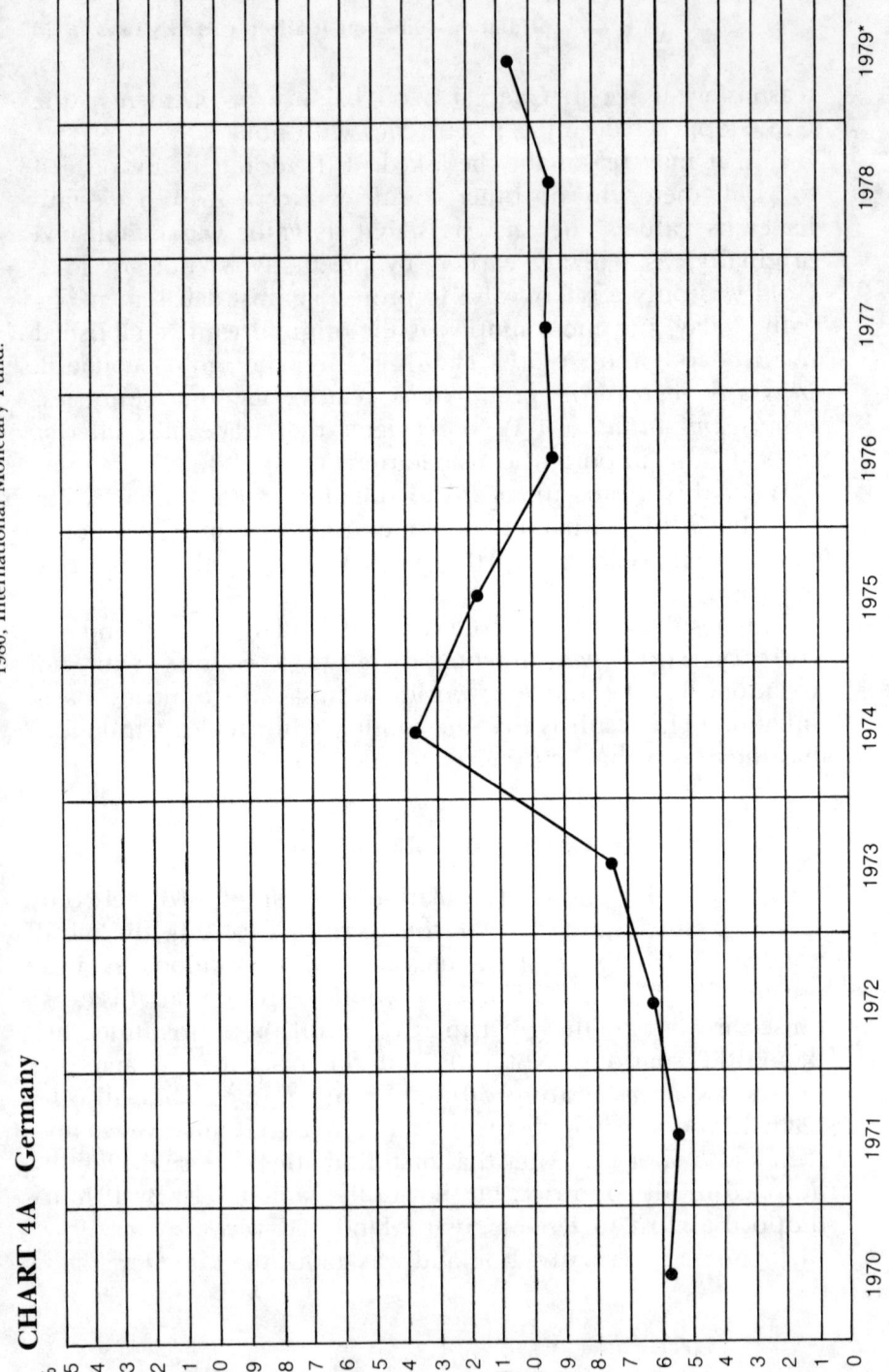

CHART 4B France

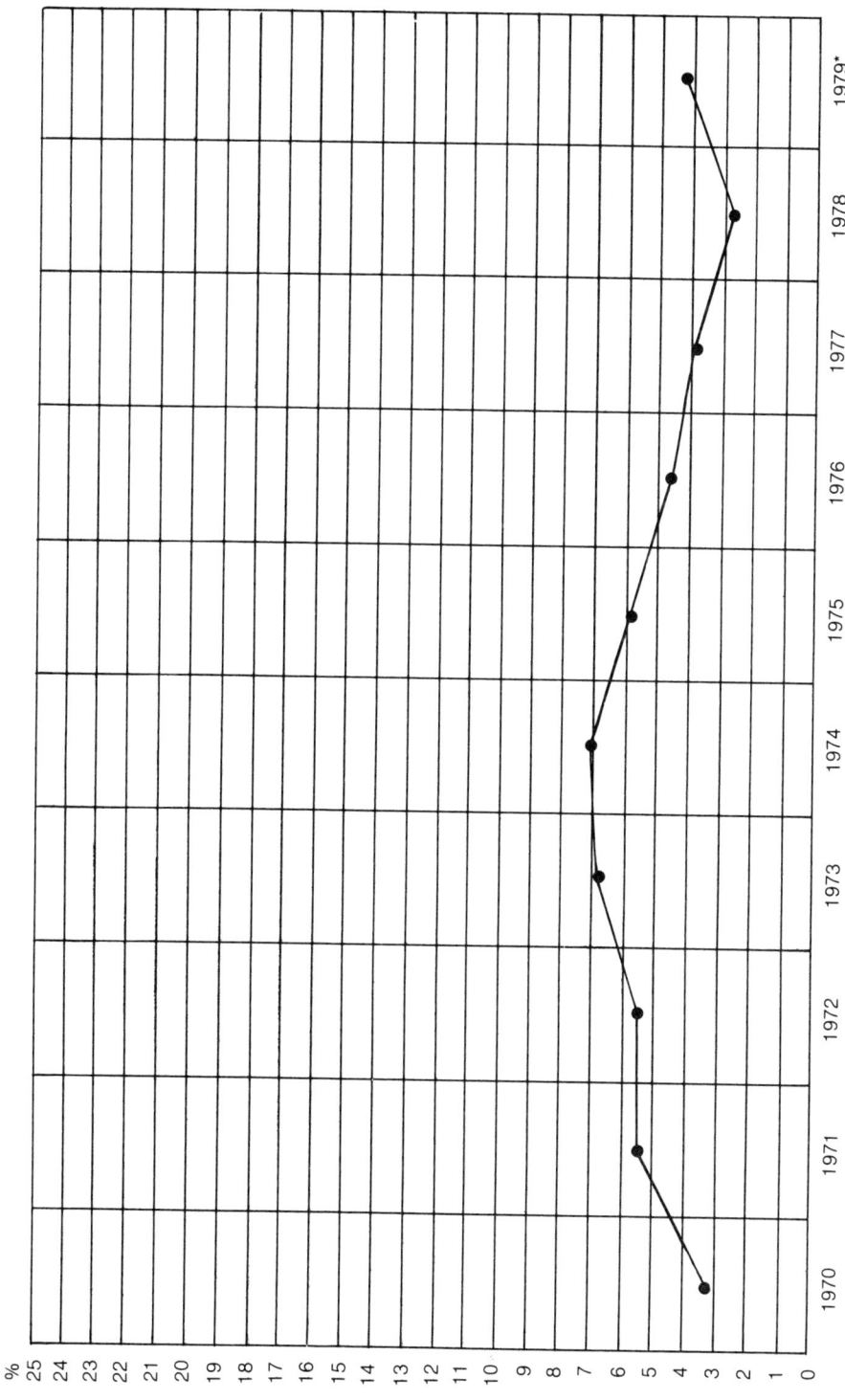

CHART 4C England

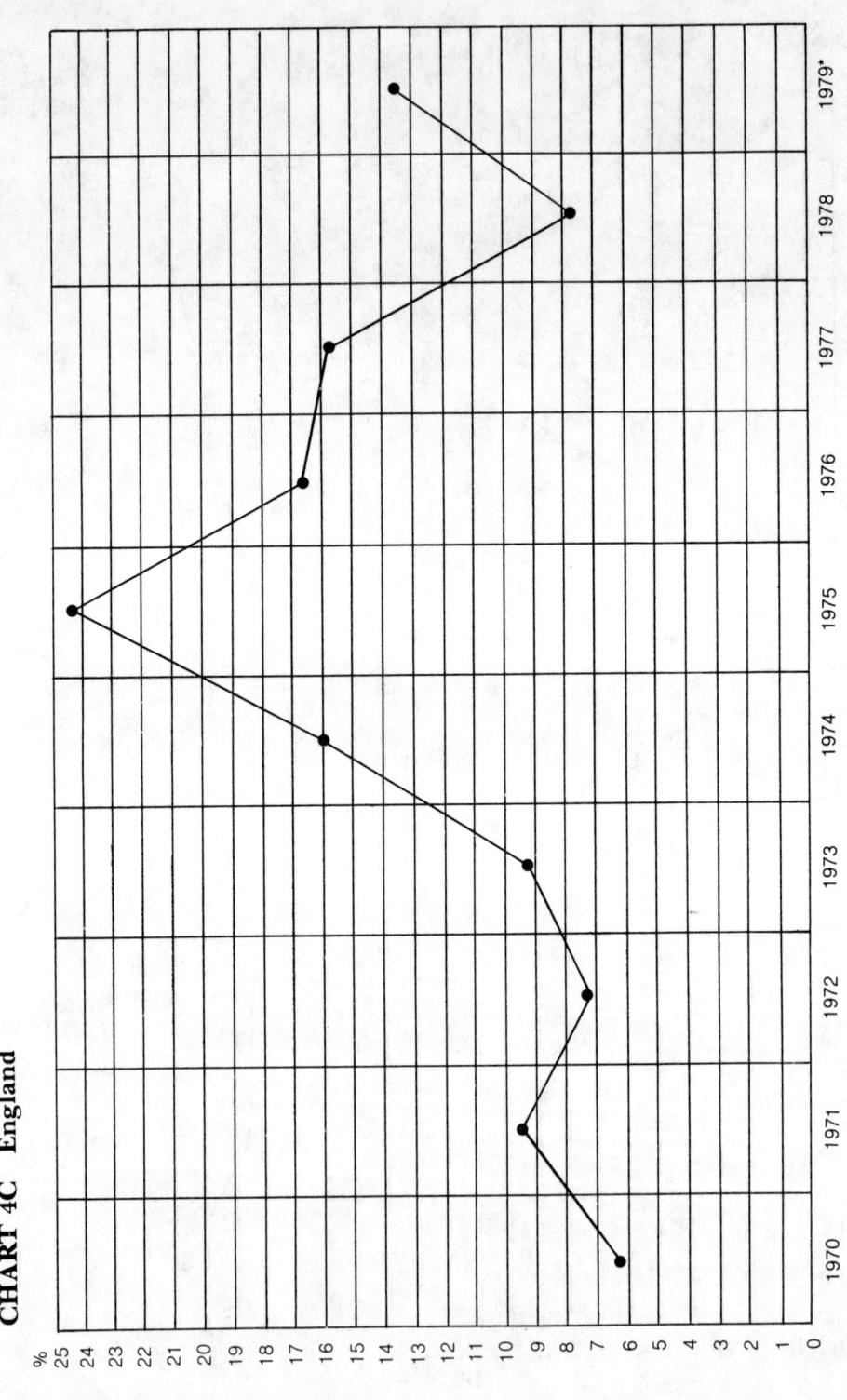

CHART 4D Canada

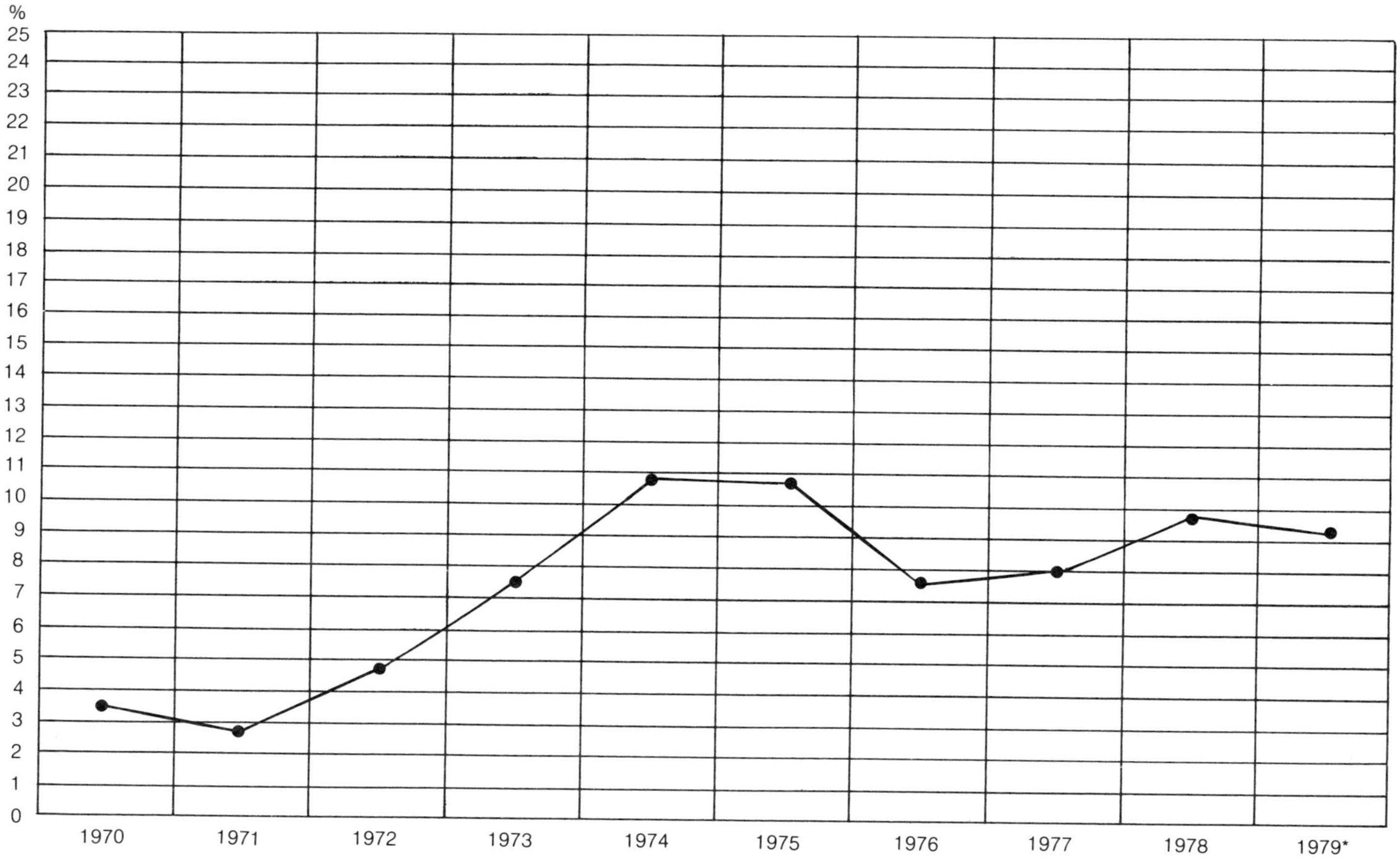

CHART 4E Switzerland

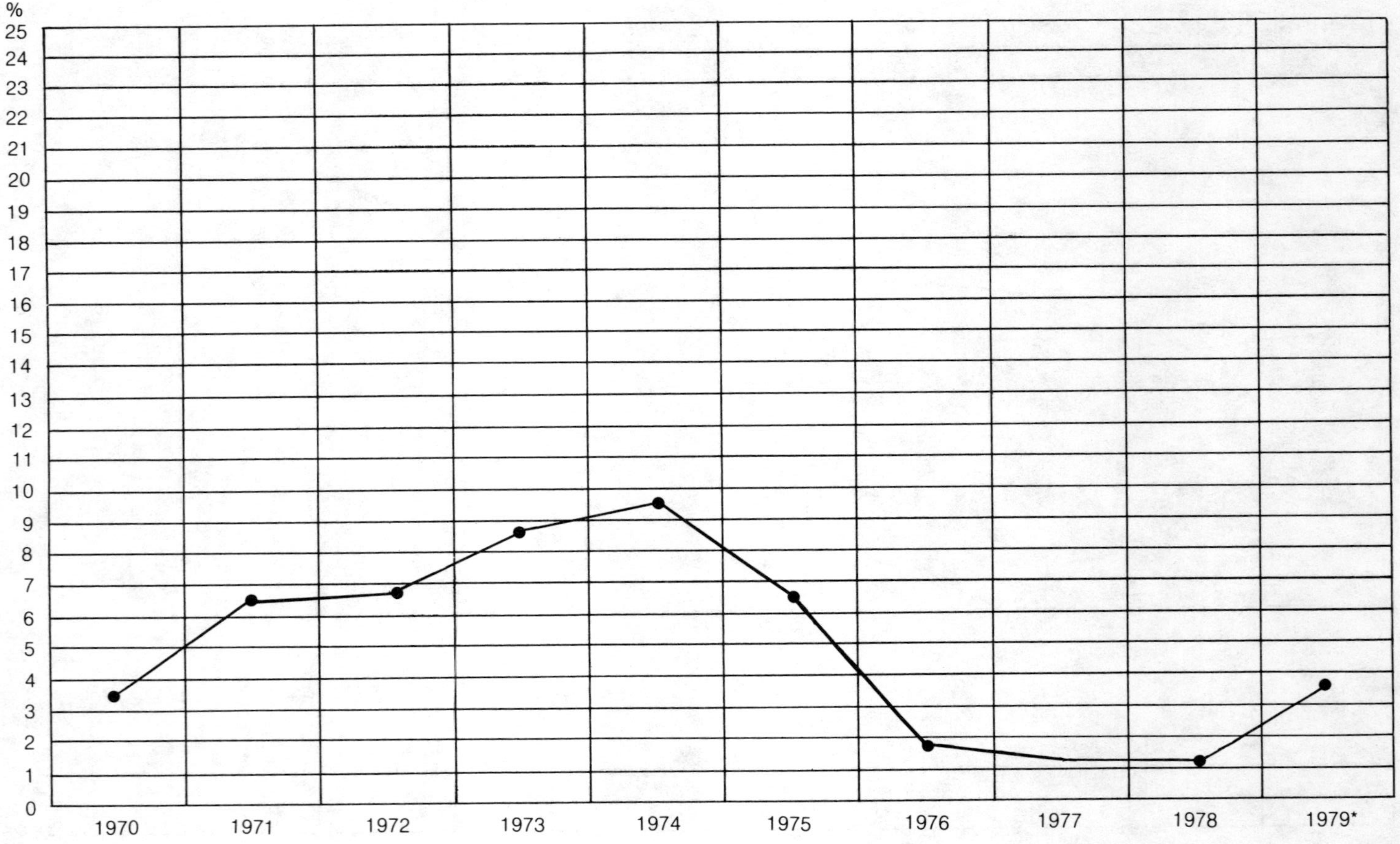

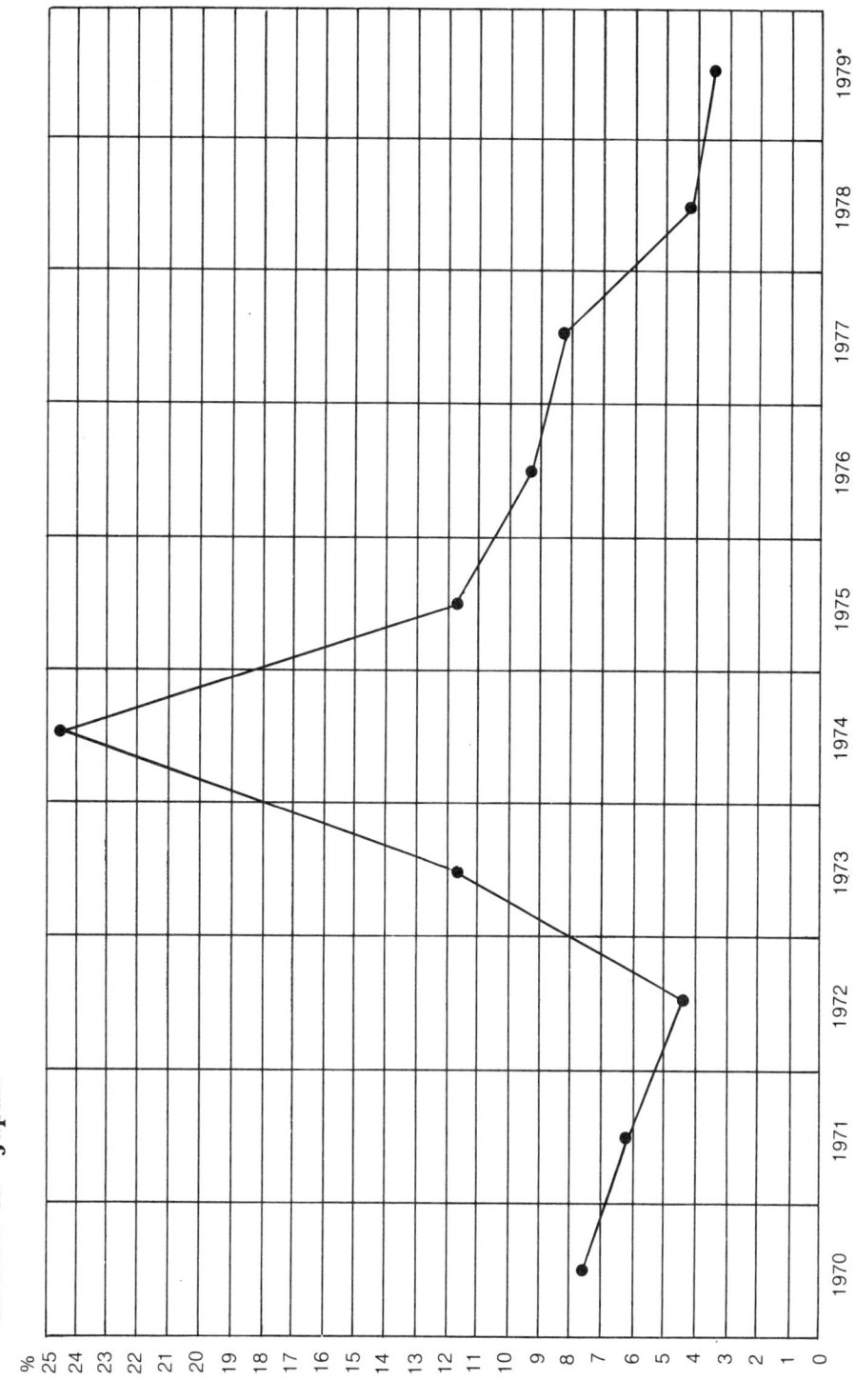

CHART 4F Japan

CHART 4G United States

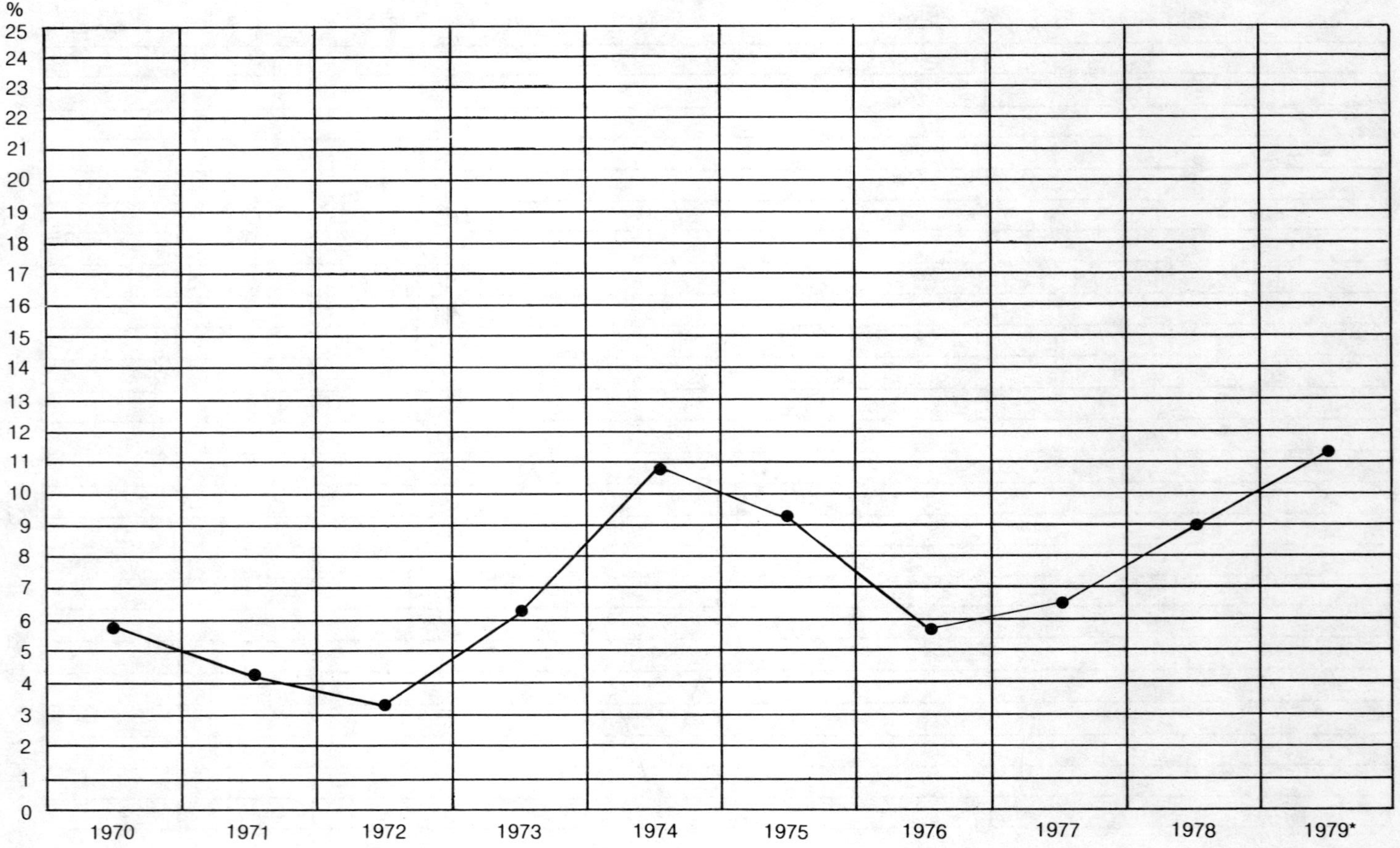

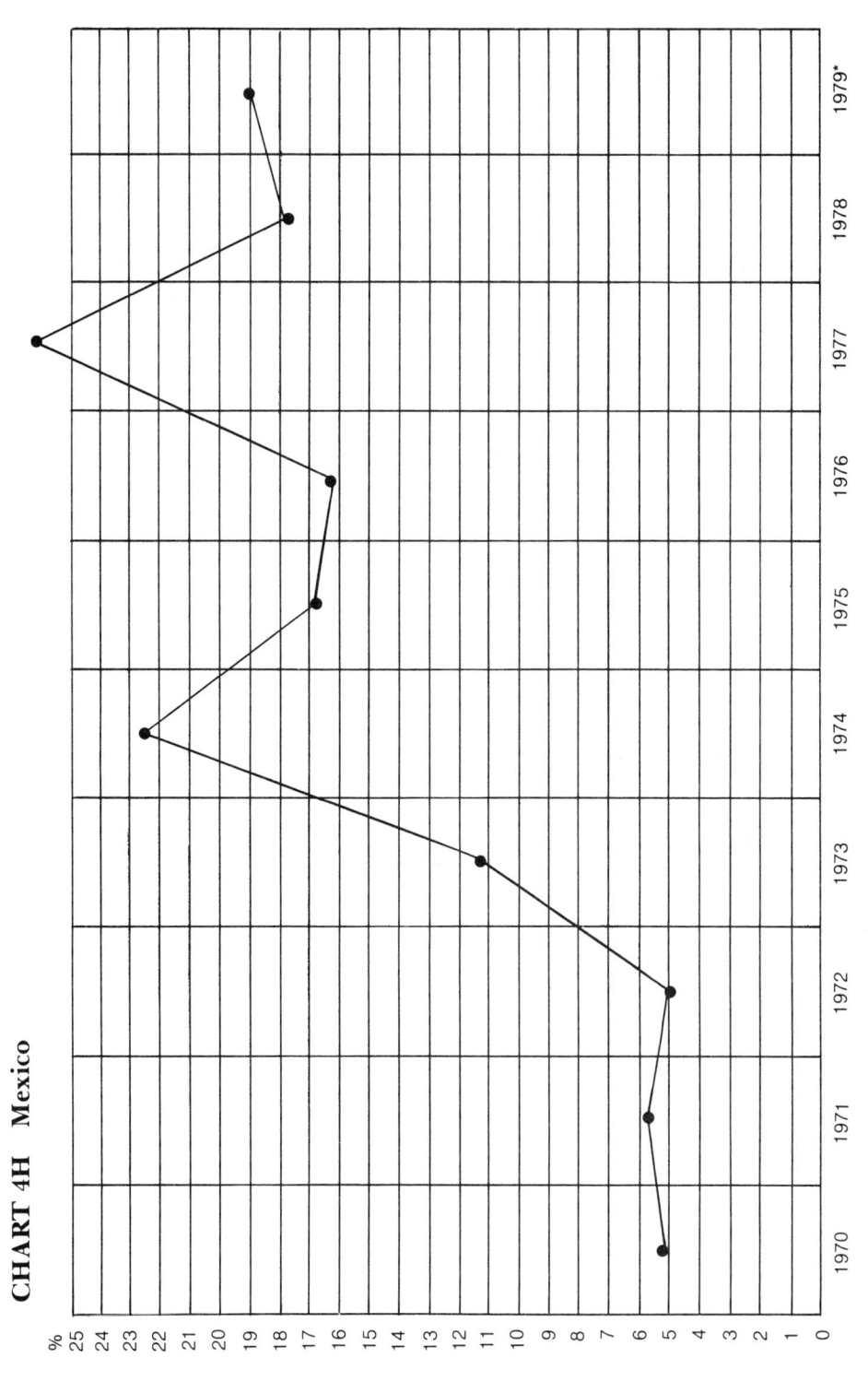

CHART 4H Mexico

the U.S., with France and Canada higher. Interestingly enough, this corresponds very closely to the values of currencies for various countries. In 1978 the Swiss franc, the mark, and the yen rose strongly against the dollar. The pound remained fairly constant while the Canadian dollar (remember, Canada had a higher inflation rate) dropped. The French franc rose slightly in spite of a mildly higher inflation rate in France than in the U.S.

When a comparison is made of currency prices going back three years, the correlation is striking. Currencies tend to fluctuate inversely in proportion to a country's rate of inflation. The relationship is unmistakable, but it is not 100 percent direct. There are periods in all currencies when in the short run the relationship does not correlate with inflation. This is why great care must be taken *not* to try to correlate price inflation with currency values in the short run. In the long run we've seen that it can be very helpful, but in the short run it can be ruinous.

Purchasing Power Parity (PPP) and the rule of one price

At this point a few words need to be said about PPP or Purchasing Power Parity, which has been promoted of late as a panacea for understanding currency exchange. PPP is a view that probably first emerged in the last century and holds that exchange rates adjust *exactly* in relation to price inflation in different countries. It is easiest to see what PPP means by taking an example.

Let's go back to our manufacturer of Japanese cars. You'll recall that he was selling his cars for 800,000 yen in Japan and $4,000 in the U.S. The exchange rate being 200 yen to one dollar, everything works out very nicely. But, now let's suppose that the U.S. has an inflation rate 3 percent higher than that of Japan (for illustration assume the U.S. rate is 3 percent, Japan is 0 percent). This means that at the end of a year, it takes $4,120 to buy what $4,000 bought a year earlier.

Inflation—and how it affects currency rates 61

The Japanese car should be now selling for $4,120 in the U.S. but still 800,000 yen in Japan (where, we've assumed, there is no inflation). If it's the same car, however, and the exchange rate remains constant, that means that the Japanese manufacturer can take the $4,120 he makes from selling the car in America, turn it in for Japanese yen at 200 to 1 (which was the exchange rate) and receive back 824,000 yen. He makes 24,000 yen by selling the car in the United States.

Something is obviously wrong here. Compensating for inflation, the car should cost the same in both countries. What's wrong is the exchange rate. The exchange rate should reflect the changing value of the currencies caused by inflation. The new rate should take, in this example, 4,120 U.S. dollars and divide it into 800,000 yen and we would find out that the proper exchange rate is not 200 yen to 1 dollar but 194 yen to 1 dollar. Of course, we don't just do it for one car, but for all products as measured by, for example, the Consumer Price Index. This relates inflation to currency rates. By checking one, we can quickly determine the other. By knowing what inflation is doing in two countries, presumably, we should be able to determine their *correct* currency relationship. If the current currency rate is different from our determined rate, we should be able to make a profit by buying the undervalued currency (or selling the overvalued one—see Chapter 10 on selling short).

Can determining true currency relationships and making a profit on them really be this simple?

It makes a convincing argument. Unfortunately, it's simply not the way things work. We have seen that inflation, like productivity, has an important relationship to currency *in the long run*. What PPP tries to do is tack that relationship down in the short run.

It's similar to a theory called "The Law of One Price." The "Law of One Price" theory in economics states that all items cost the same amount, except for transportation charges, anywhere in the world. While it is generally true for raw commodities such as wheat or orange juice, it is definitely false, as we shall soon see, for manufactured goods.

Let's consider our car manufacturer again, only this time in Japan. It costs something to get the product here to the United States. There are preparation charges in getting the car ready for shipment. There are dock loading, shipping, and unloading expenses. And then there is the cost of getting the car ready once it arrives (removing protective coatings, etc.).

These charges are substantial. We'll guess that they amount to $500 a car. (In actuality they are probably somewhat less.) Now consider this cost from the Japanese manufacturer's viewpoint. In Japan he produces a range of cars from "stripped" to "loaded." The stripped car sells for 400,000 yen in Japan, the loaded car for 700,000 yen. Yet, it costs exactly $500 (100,000 yen) to send either car. It costs no more to ship the expensive car than the cheap car in dollars (or yen). Yet the shipping costs expressed as a percentage of total car costs is less for the expensive car. Consider:

400,000 cheap car
<u>100,000</u> shipping
500,000 total   Shipping is 20 percent of total cost

700,000 expensive car
<u>100,000</u> shipping
800,000 total   Shipping is 12 percent of total cost

From this viewpoint it's cheaper to ship the more expensive car than the less expensive one. From a competitive point of view, the foreign (American) buyer is less likely to object paying 12 percent of total cost for shipping than paying 20 percent of total cost.

This, in fact, is what happens. That's why the best and most expensive Florida and California fruit end up in New York and the best and most expensive European exports end up in California. And why the more expensive Japanese car is sent to America.

Inflation—and how it affects currency rates 63

However, as we saw in Chapter 1 with demand curves, more people will buy a product when the price is lower. The Japanese manufacturer will sell a plentitude of cars in Japan at 400,000 yen, but very few at 700,000 yen. Yet, he may sell a plentitude of cars costing 800,000 yen (700,000 cost plus 100,000 shipping) or $4,000 in the U.S., if U.S. car manufacturers are not as efficient. (For them a low-cost car manufactured in the U.S. may be $5,000.)

The higher priced car in Japan becomes the lower priced car in the U.S., and the Japanese manufacturer makes a bundle of money selling *two different* cars in two different markets.

The problems with PPP should be coming into focus. In general, manufacturers do not offer the exact same product both at home and in foreign markets; they offer different products. So price comparisons of domestic and foreign consumed products are, at best, guesses.

In addition, even if an inflation were to occur, as we suggested, of 3 percent or $120, this does not mean that the Japanese manufacturer would necessarily increase his price in the U.S. He might make up the $120 by increased efficiency on the models sold in America (or increased costs of the models sold in Japan). Or he might change them slightly, coming up with a different and lower priced mixture. Or, he might cut back on his product's quality, or he might encourage his dealers to be more courteous and offer better service and raise the price only $20 instead of the inflationary required $120. All this, in fact, is exactly what Japanese car manufacturers did when inflation in the U.S. outpaced inflation in Japan.

Finally, if these problems did not exist there still is the problem of determining what inflation index to use in determining PPP. Is it the CPI we've been using? Or is it the Wholesale Price Index (WPI)? Some have suggested using an Export Price Index or a Unit Labor Cost Index. If we were to compare these four different indices we would find that at any given time, they all show different amounts and rates. The problem is that there really is no one true index to be followed.

Inflation/interest rate trade-off

One other interesting phenomenon occurs between countries with different inflation rates. The country with the lower inflation rate tends to attract investment money from banks, wealthy private individuals, and multi-national companies. The reason for this is quite simple. Let's go back to our example of Japan and the U.S., which assumed that Japan has a 0 percent inflation rate while that of the U.S. is 3 percent.

We'll further assume that interest rates in both Japan and the United States are 7 percent. A person putting money in a Japanese bank at 0 percent inflation will earn a true 7 percent on that money. A person putting money in a 7 percent interest account in a U.S. bank, however, will earn only 4 percent interest on the money. The other 3 percent interest has been lost to inflation.

One would think that a disparity between interest rates in various countries would tend not to occur. In order to attract money investors, the U.S. would necessarily have to raise its interest rates, in our example. In general this is true. In the case of the United States, it is not. Banks in this country are limited in the interest they may pay on savings accounts. Until 1978 that interest rate was about 7½ percent maximum on long-term deposits. People who could not go out of the country would deposit their money at those rates because they had no alternative. This even though inflation might be 9½ percent and their deposit was losing 2 percent annually!

For a time the U.S.'s artificially low interest rates attracted investors. But eventually, large investors went abroad for higher real interest rate returns. When investment money chases high interest rates it has an effect on currency. Investors leaving a country trade off that country's currency, thereby adding to downward pressure on the currency. Investors entering a country trade for its currency, adding to upward pressure. When too many investors (including large American financial and business institutions) went abroad, it helped send the dollar down.

The U.S. was forced to raise its interest rates. Banks and savings and loan associations began offering Treasury Bill accounts paying 10 percent annually and higher. The discount rate charged by the federal reserve to its member banks soared to 12 percent and the prime rate, which banks charge their preferred institutional customers, rose even higher.

The lesson to be learned here is that low interest rates and high inflation do not mix. If they do, currency will be negatively affected and those in the know can take advantage of the situation.

5

Balance of payments—how to use it as a currency indicator

THE SINGLE BEST PROGNOSTICATOR of currency rates is the Balance of Payments (BOP). It has been my experience (and that of many other currency watchers) that the BOP has, in the past, reliably indicated future currency trends. This is not to say, however, that the BOP does not have its detractors. There are some who argue that, for reasons we shall discuss shortly, the BOP is virtually useless. As we'll see, their arguments have some merit, but first let's consider just what the BOP actually is.

The dollar after World War II

In 1944 with World War II winding down, the major industrialized nations of the west met at Bretton Woods in New Hampshire and created the International Monetary Fund (IMF). One purpose of the IMF was to maintain stability of currencies after the war. To be avoided were the wild infla-

Balance of payments as a currency indicator 67

tions which occurred after World War I (particularly in Germany) and which, some have argued, caused the economic chaos that led to World War II.

In 1944 the strongest country, economically, in the world was the United States. It was decided at the Bretton Woods meeting that the U.S. would officially peg its currency at $35 per ounce of gold. Upon demand of foreigners, the U.S. would unquestioningly exchange $35 US for an ounce of the precious metal. (At that time U.S. citizens were prohibited from owning gold.)

The effect of this decision was to make the U.S. dollar the world's reserve currency; it was the basic currency used in trade. All other currencies were weaker than the U.S. dollar.

For a while this worked to the advantage of the U.S. As it turned out, the war-ravaged countries of Europe badly needed U.S. products, but they had few U.S. dollars to buy these goods with. Without dollars, they could not make purchases from the U.S. This problem reached crisis proportions in the late 1940s and terms such as the "dollar gap" and the "dollar shortage" were bandied about by news commentators. (Note: This is the opposite of the "dollar glut" we hear so much about today.)

When the war-torn countries tried to make purchases, they found they had trouble converting their own currencies into dollars. They had little to export and they needed great quantities of imports. Consequently, all the European countries were competing to exchange their own currencies for dollars. European currencies became unwanted.* As increasing numbers of marks and francs and lira were turned in for dollars, fewer and fewer people wanted foreign currency. In order to maintain the value of their own currencies, foreign governments purchased their own money back from the U.S. with gold. By the end of the 1940s, the U.S. had over three-

---

*In actual practice dollars are not always physically exchanged for foreign currency. Rather, dollar deposits in U.S. banks by foreigners are reduced while deposits held by U.S. banks in other countries are increased.

quarters of the free world's supply of gold. It is important to understand that the U.S. built up this gold supply by exporting more than it imported. The U.S. had a surplus balance of trade while foreign governments had a shortage or deficit.

The role of foreign investment

If, however, this condition had continued indefinitely, at some point the U.S. would have acquired all the free world's gold, and foreign countries would have found it impossible to purchase anything more (unless we accepted some other form of wealth). Actually, the exchange of gold for currency is only a short-term solution to the trade problem. One long-term solution is foreign investment.

During the later 1940s when the U.S. was receiving so much foreign currency, one method of returning this money to foreign countries without the use of gold was for U.S. companies to invest abroad. When a U.S. tire company, for example, opened up a factory in France, it had to pay for land, the construction of the buildings, and the labor force in francs. It got the francs by converting dollars. This brought more dollars to France and eased the trade deficit that France was having with the U.S. at the time.

France bought U.S. goods by converting francs into dollars. U.S. companies invested in France by converting dollars into francs. It was a mutually beneficial arrangement.

Early impact of foreign aid

There was yet another method of providing dollars to needy countries abroad—giving them away. This took the form of unilateral aid. Through the Marshall Plan, the U.S. simply gave away dollars, food, and other merchandise without expecting anything in return. It has been estimated by some that this last method was by far the most effective in putting Europe and Japan back on their feet, economically speaking, after the War.

BOP accounting

When we take into account all the items that contributed to getting more dollars overseas to fill the "dollar gap," we get the following list:

1. Merchandise and services that we *import* (trade dollars for foreign currencies to pay for this)
2. Gold that we *receive* (for dollars)
3. Capital investments that *we make* in foreign countries
4. Direct unilateral grants of aid

These four items send dollars overseas. However, as we noted earlier, we get foreign currencies back (although not as many in the late 1940 period we are discussing). Here is a list of items that bring dollars back to the United States:

1. Merchandise and services that we *export* (foreign countries trade their currency for U.S. dollars to pay for this)
2. Gold that we *pay out* (for currency)
3. Investments of *foreigners* here (short-term)
4. Capital investments by foreigners (The U.S. does not receive foreign aid grants.)

If these items are placed next to each other, they form a bookkeeping system:

	Credits U.S. receives foreign currency	**Debits** U.S. pays out dollars
Merchandise and services	exports	imports
Gold	for dollars	for foreign currencies
Investments (short term)	by foreigners here	by Americans abroad
Capital investments		
Foreign aid	—————	unilateral payments
total	$?	$?

When we add the total credits, then the total debits and compare the figures we would expect that they would balance out. They did for a number of years as gold transferred hands to make up for shortages or surpluses in other areas.

One area of the bookkeeping that almost never balances, however, and which is of great importance to us, is the part dealing with merchandise and services. This, as we've said, has to do with importing and exporting—trade. It is the item which, because of its size, is what gold and investment tend to balance out, not the other way around.

The current account

Trade and short-term investments are sometimes called the "current account." It is the critical part of the balance of payments calculation. When there is a current account surplus, it means that more is exported than imported and there is gold coming into the country to make up for the difference. (Investment in foreign countries does not react quickly to follow the current account status.) When there is a current account deficit, imports exceed exports and gold is going out.

As noted, for a number of years after World War II, this method of totaling up credits and debits worked well for the U.S. We regularly had far more on the credit side and received gold.

After the 1950s, however, things began to go the other way for the U.S. Foreign economies just coming to life had brand-new equipment to work with and big incentives to get rich like their American cousins. Soon, foreign countries were producing many products that consumers in the United States wanted including watches, cameras, and automobiles. As we bought these products, they increased our imports. Soon the current account was no longer lopsided in our favor.

Foreign capital investment also was out of balance. Foreigners did not invest in the U.S. (until recently) at anything like the rate we were investing abroad. In addition, U.S. grants of unilateral foreign aid (and the cost of maintaining U.S. soldiers in foreign countries such as Korea and Germany) meant free dollars given to foreign governments. Finally, there was the problem of U.S. inflation.

As we saw in Chapter 4, for a number of years the rate of inflation in the U.S. was comparatively high. This meant that even though trade might be balanced, we were paying with dollars worth less than the currency they were being exchanged for (in terms of buying power at home). The imbalance in total payments and the pressure of inflation resulted in the dollar becoming less desirable. This, in turn, was expressed as an increased demand for foreign currencies. But, the ratio of exchange had been fixed at Bretton Woods and did not change. It was maintained by the agreement which stipulated that foreigners could always trade in U.S. dollars for gold at the rate of $35 per ounce. Our money continued to be gladly accepted.

Devaluation of the dollar

The problem, however, was that the U.S., like other countries, could not forever go on selling gold without eventually running out. The tide turned about 1960 (see Chart 5A).

Note the early years when we took in gold so other countries would have dollars to spend. Then note the decline from 1960 when we gave foreign countries gold so that they would accept our dollars.

It is apparent from this chart that by 1970 our gold supplies were getting low. Consequently, in a bold move, the U.S. in 1971 devalued the dollar. The meeting was at the Smithsonian Institution and the result was that the U.S. dollar would be redeemed with less gold and the IMF would allow greater flexibility in meeting par values. While this slowed the loss of gold, it did not solve the problem. Soon there was an additional devaluation until finally the U.S. stopped paying out gold at all for the dollar. We were off the gold standard by

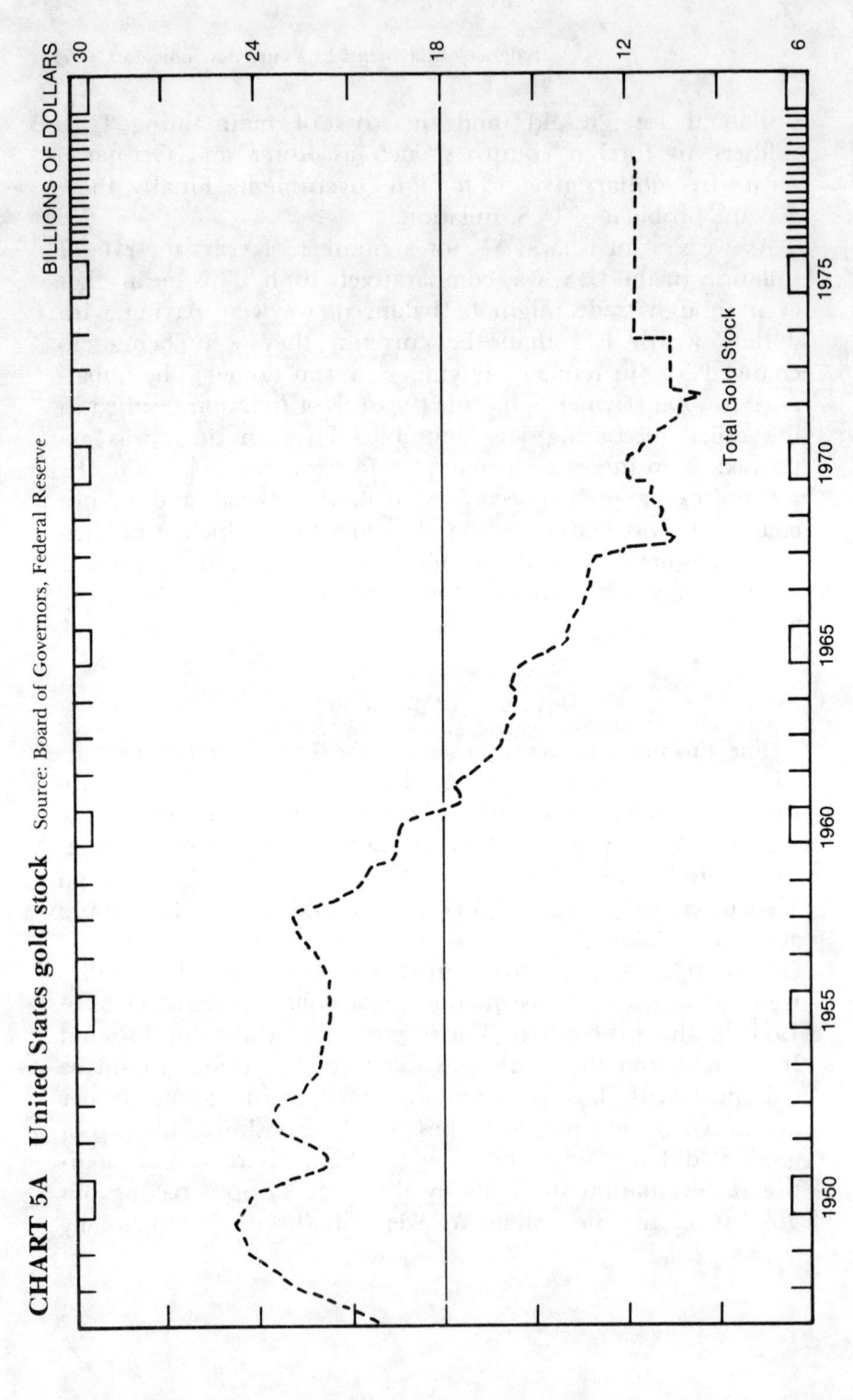

CHART 5A United States gold stock Source: Board of Governors, Federal Reserve

1973. [For a time there was an exchange of gold between the central banks of foreign countries and the U.S., but Special Drawing Rights (SDR) have taken the place of this.]

Now the U.S had an apparent solution to its problem. We simply wouldn't redeem our paper currency with gold. Unfortunately, the solution was in reality a castastrophe for the U.S. dollar, as can be seen by Chart 5B. This shows the value of the U.S. dollar against a group of important foreign currencies through 1978. (The dollar rebounded in late 1979.)

CHART 5B Foreign currency price of United States dollar

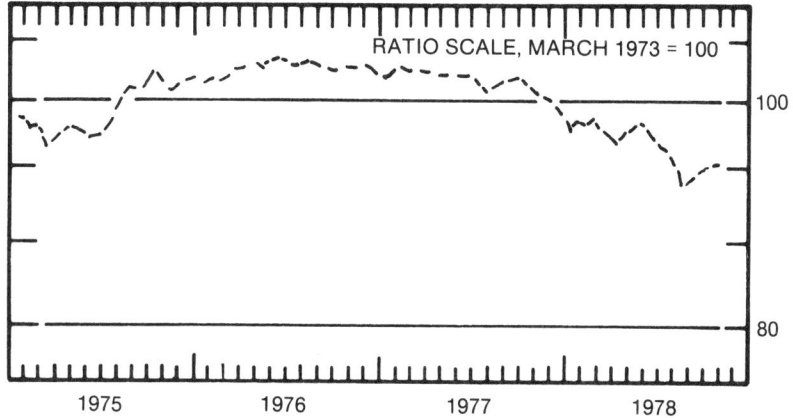

When the U.S. stopped redeeming its paper money with gold, there was a period of stability as the dollar found its natural level relative to other currencies. But, when the current account began to show we were no longer exporting more than importing, the dollar's stability came into question. When we finally began importing more than exporting, we needed more foreign currency to pay for our imports. We sold dollars to get it and the pressure downward on the dollar increased. In the past this downward pressure was compensated for by gold. But the U.S. now refused to redeem its dollars in gold. The result was an increasingly abrupt descent in the dollar's value relative to other currencies. The current account's recent history is shown on Chart 5C for comparison to the dollar's fall. Note that the deficit in the current account presaged the time and the amount of the 1978 fall of the dollar.

CHART 5C The current account

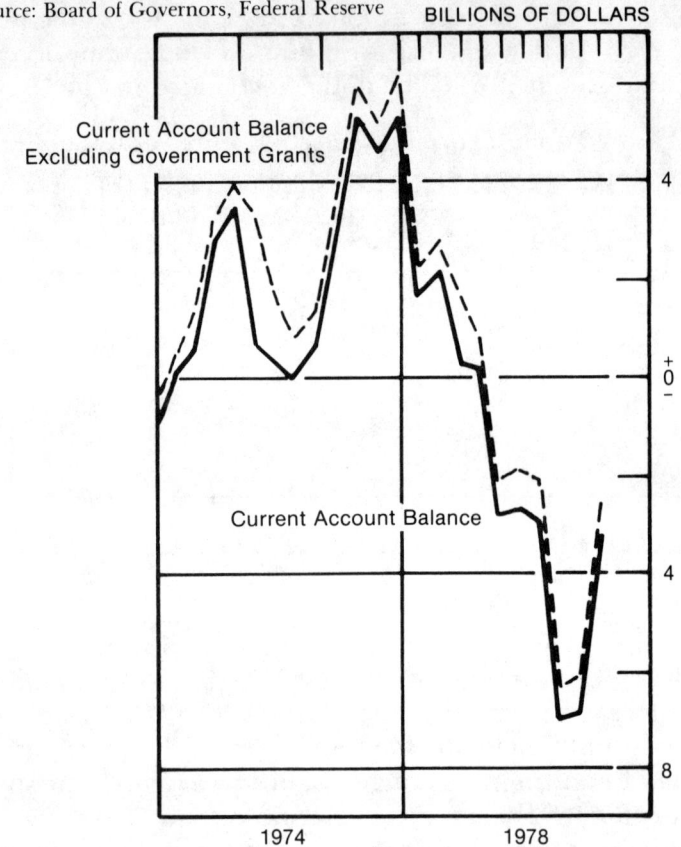

It has been my observation that current account deficits tend to create additional downward pressure on the dollar while current account surpluses (for the U.S.) help the dollar. The important point here is that the current account tends to lead the dollar trend, not the other way around. This is most clearly seen when the U.S. announces the current account near the end of each month. The figures announced are for an account that has already been closed, so the account itself, at the time of the announcement, could not be affected by currency rates. Currency rates, however, dip or rise upon account news. They are affected by it. An unusually large dip often produces selling of the U.S. dollar as investors anticipate new downward pressure. Unusually small deficits or surpluses have the opposite effect. (See Chapter 7 for a discussion of "anticipation.")

The effect is long-term as well as short-term. Persistent current account deficits are reflected in persistent declines of the dollar. When the current account shows a balance or a surplus for an extended period of time, currency rates, as we have seen, tend to favor the dollar.

A word of caution is in order here. The reader should not draw the conclusion that the current account is a panacea when trying to figure out what currency is going to do. It is not. It should only be considered as one of many indicators. In addition, the reader should be aware that there are some knowledgeable people who dispute the prognosticating powers of the BOP.

Intervention

Most of the arguments I've seen against the BOP have to do with a single word, intervention. Intervention sounds nasty and in a sense it is. Before we can understand the criticism against the BOP, we must come to an understanding of what this word encompasses.

What intervention amounts to is the attempt by governments to control the free market exchange of currency by utilizing their central banks. (The U.S. central bank is the Federal Reserve.) Central banks buy up U.S. dollars, when the dollar is falling, by exchanging their own currencies for them.

This has the effect of depressing the value of foreign currency and increasing the value of U.S. dollars. The banks intervene to help or prop up the dollar.

Why would the central banks of foreign countries be so generous?

Foreign governments know that the single biggest consumer market in the western world is the United States. In order to thrive, in some cases in order to survive, foreign companies must sell in the U.S. But, as the price of foreign currencies increases and that of the U.S. dollar drops, it becomes increasingly difficult for foreigners to sell here. Consider the case of transistor radios. When the Japanese yen was 300 to one dollar and it cost 6,000 yen for a Japanese radio, that radio in the U.S. could be expected to sell for about $20. But, when the yen dropped to 200 to one, the U.S. price for the Japanese radio shot up to $30. Of course, as we noted earlier, products are not always the same in different countries. Companies absorb some of the loss, change their quality, and so on. (See Chapter 3.) Nevertheless, eventually the change in exchange rates is going to hurt the sale of Japanese radios in the U.S. because of the fact that they will eventually cost more. An extreme example helps make the point. Consider what would happen if the exchange rate dropped to 20 yen to one dollar. Now the radio that formerly cost $20 would cost $300. The Japanese company would not be able to sell its radios in the U.S. market. It would cut back its labor force, reduce its use of raw materials, and might even go bankrupt. To prevent this from happening and threatening its economy is why foreign central banks intervene and prop up the dollar.

As an aside, we should keep in mind that this intervention is an "artificial" process. It is natural for trade, productivity, inflation, and interest rates to exert their influence. It is natural for currency rates to follow. If there is no intervention, an equilibrium can be achieved.

Consider trade: As the price of foreign goods rises, we tend to buy less of them. This reduces our imports and the exports to us from foreign countries. That means that fewer dollars go out. If we have a balance of payments deficit, fewer dollars out helps to bring it back into line. On the other hand, the action of central banks intervening by buying dollars to prop up the dollar defeats this natural function. The dollar is artificially propped up. Eventually, the banks run out of determination or resources and the props fall . . . and so does the dollar. Usually, however, because intervention has held back the fall for an unnatural period of time, the dollar plunges further and faster than it would if there had been no intervention at all.

Intervention and the BOP

Intervention may have a direct impact on our measurement of the BOP. You'll recall we said that the BOP is composed primarily of trade and investment. Let's consider for a moment how these are measured. Of course, we could get the figures from every importer and exporter, but this would require an enormous bureaucracy. There is an easier way available.

Every time we import a camera we trade dollars for marks, yen, or whatever. Currently, we import more than we export and there is a surplus of dollars overseas. These excess dollars show up at foreign banks where exporters exchange currency. The banks turn over the excess dollars to their country's central bank, which may eventually redeem it with the U.S. central bank. Each month (that we import more than we export) there should be excess dollars accumulated at the central banks of foreign countries. Consequently, if we measure the change in reserves of foreign central banks, we should know how much our trade imports are out of line with our exports in terms of dollars. The U.S. balance of trade deficit could be found by comparing the monthly change in the reserves of foreign central banks. Of course, these banks also handle investments (both short and long) as well as trade. Consequently, the change in reserves could be used to measure the total BOP deficit or surplus.

78 Buying and selling currency for profit

In actual practice, since it is extremely difficult to accurately measure all trade transactions (not to mention foreign investments), changes in foreign central bank reserves are used to finalize the BOP. They are the bottom line. Consider this example:

Assume that the following changes occurred in a single month.

Japan increased U.S. dollar reserves	$1 billion U.S.
Germany increased U.S. dollar reserves	$1 billion U.S.
Switzerland increased U.S. dollar reserves	$200 million U.S.
total	$2.2 billion

If we assumed that all other countries balanced out, the U.S. balance of payments deficit could be presumed to be 2.2 billion dollars.

Now, of course, comes the objection to this system of measurement. Central banks of foreign countries intervene on a regular basis. Their intervention shows up as a purchase of U.S. dollars and sale of their own currencies. Consider what would happen if in the next month, the following countries intervened:

Japan's intervention	$1 billion U.S.
Germany's intervention	$1 billion U.S.
Switzerland's intervention	$200 million U.S.
total	$2.2 billion

The intervention exactly equalled the changes in reserves of the previous month. Now let's further assume that in the first month there was no intervention and in the second month there was no trade and investment imbalance. How would we know the difference between BOP imbalance and intervention between the two months? Both months show exactly the same total change in foreign reserves, $2.2 billion U.S.! Our measuring stick doesn't tell us. We only know the amount, not if it's "oil or water."

From this argument it is easy to see why some feel that the BOP is not a reliable indicator. If anything, people who hold this argument usually say that the BOP is an indication of how determined foreign governments are to prop up the U.S. dollar. (Note: the U.S. government began active intervention in 1978.) They argue that rather than show where the dollar is likely to fall in the future, it shows how much effort is being made to keep the dollar where it is today.

While this argument is very appealing, it holds very little water. To begin with, the part of the BOP measurement that is or should be used to indicate imbalance is the current account. It shows import/export figures (and short-term investment), but not other capital investment. It is calculated using figures reported by large financial institutions and is only moderately influenced by foreign central bank reserve changes.

In addition, one must ask again, why would a foreign central bank choose to intervene? The reason must be that there is real downward pressure on the dollar. If the BOP were in equilibrium, inflation and productivity balanced, presumably no central bank would have the incentive to intervene. (It might be argued that intervention could be undertaken to drive the value of a foreign currency even higher against a stable dollar in order to create more trading opportunities. This is highly unlikely given the state of the world economy today.)

The central banks of foreign governments intervene because there *is* real downward pressure on the dollar. They intervene almost every time the dollar drops. The West German Bundesbank reported that its intervention in 1978 alone totaled $24 billion U.S. and that overall intervention that year ran as high as $50 billion U.S.

Does this mean that the Balance of Payments measurement is inaccurate? Yes and no. It's not as accurate as I or any other reasonable person would like. But, it's not completely off, either. Remember, massive intervention can mean only one thing—the dollar has enormous pressure on it. Intervention in itself is another indicator that the dollar is in trouble. Unfortunately, central banks only announce their intervention long after it has happened, if they announce it at all.

CHART 5D United States International Transactions (Census basis:

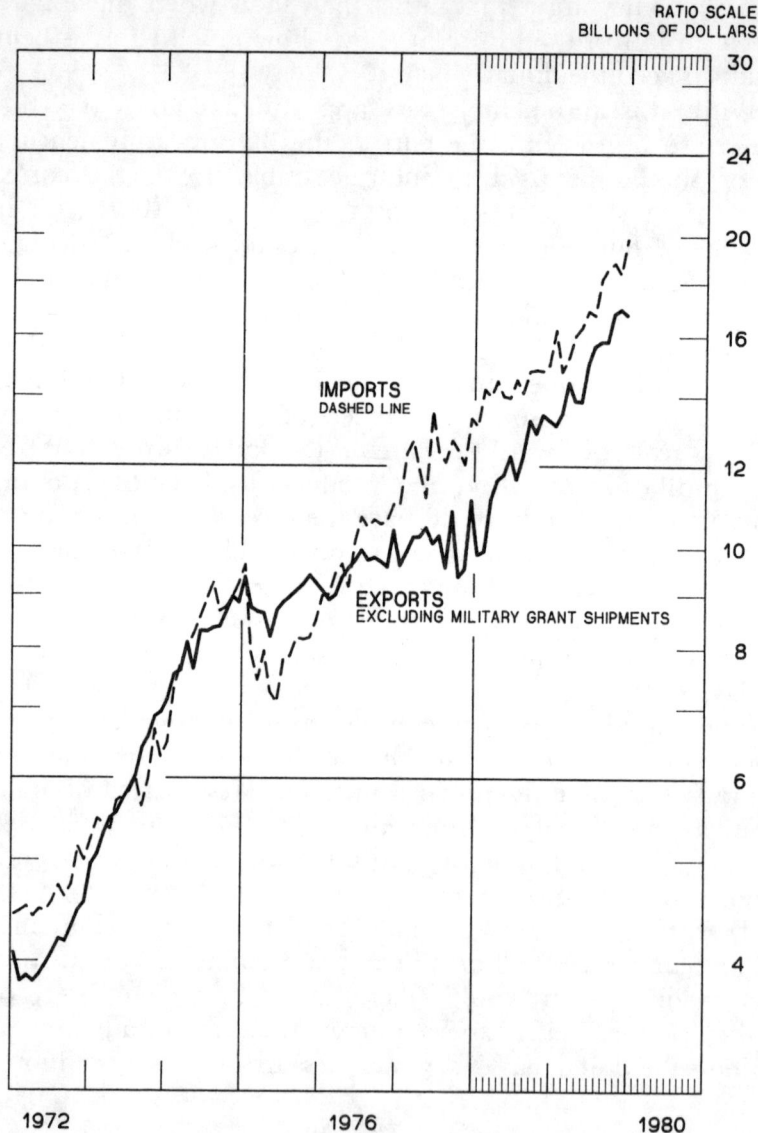

seasonally adjusted, monthly) Source: Board of Governors, Federal Reserve

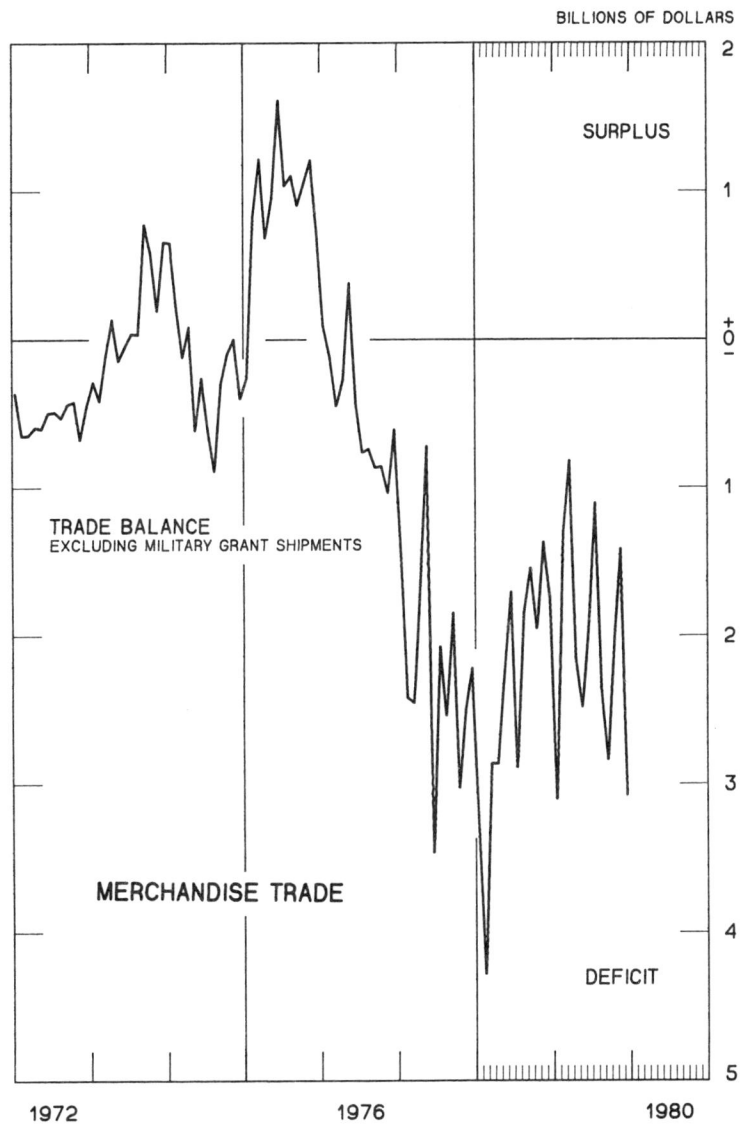

6

Petrodollars—shifting wealth away

To BE TRULY INDEPENDENT TODAY, economically speaking, a country must be industrialized, must produce food, and must have natural resources. Fortunately, almost no country possesses all three. (I say fortunately because if many countries had all three, the world would be divided up into hundreds of island states with nothing to bind countries together.) In order to survive, countries must depend upon one another.

The United States probably comes the closest to being independent of any of the other world states. It has great industrial capacity; it produces so much food that it is the world's greatest food exporter; and it has enormous natural resources. Unfortunately, the United States is also probably the world's greatest consumer. While in most cases we can produce sufficient manufactured and food products to supply ourselves, we are lacking in many raw materials—natural resources.

This is not to say that the United States is a land without

natural resources. Quite the opposite is true. A hundred years ago this country had almost every known natural resource that man could want. We have, however, depleted our natural wealth. The Masabi Range, mountains virtually made out of iron, were cut down to provide steel for World War II. Forests in the Northwest were laid bare to build railroads, cities, and provide paper products (which means that today we get a high percentage of our paper products from Canada). Immense oil fields were quickly used up to provide fuel for automobile-crazy consumers.

The petrodollar effect

While the U.S. has depleted many of its natural resources, the one that always makes the headlines is oil, and that's what we'll concentrate on. At one time, the U.S. was the world's largest supplier of oil, and exported great quantities of it. Eventually, however, domestic demand caught up with supply and then surpassed it. Today, we are probably the world's largest importer of oil. (Even though we still produce about half of what we consume.)

Oil is no different from any other commodity. If we import it, we must pay for it with something. That something, of course, is dollars. Until 1974 the U.S. had little trouble paying for its oil imports with dollars. For one thing, the amount we imported tended to be a much smaller fraction of total consumption than it is today. For another, U.S. companies had developed the enormous oil fields in the Mideast and had a voice in the price of crude oil.

In 1974, however, the Organization of Petroleum Exporting Countries (OPEC), consisting primarily of the Arab nations, flexed their muscles and demanded and received huge price increases. Suddenly the U.S. was forced to pay out many more dollars than before. These became known as petrodollars.

Of course, the United States was not alone in this predicament. The industrialized nations of Europe are far more dependent on imported oil than we are. (With the possible exception of North Sea oil.)

For Europe the increase in oil prices resulted in a sudden and dramatic escalation of prices for oil-related items, which happen to be most things. You'll recall that almost all the countries of Europe showed an enormous price inflation during the 1974-1975 period as the price of oil and oil-related products forced the consumer price index higher (see discussion of inflation in Chapter 4).

After this price hike, two European countries, Germany and Switzerland, concentrated on increasing their productivity and exports, on promoting foreign investment at home, and controlling oil consumption. (Germany's oil consumption increased only about 7 percent between 1974 and 1977. Switzerland's declined about 2 percent during the same period!) For those two countries, the increase in oil prices and the subsequent inflation were quickly brought under control. Inflation dropped from 7 percent in 1974 to just 2.7 percent in 1978 in Germany; from 9.7 percent in 1974 to just over 1 percent by 1978 in Switzerland.

The rest of the world's countries, as we saw in Chapter 4, did not fare so well (with the exception of Japan). The United States did miserably. Our oil consumption between 1974 and 1978 went up over 68 percent! During that same period our rate of inflation went from 10.9 percent, down to 5.8 percent and then back up to 9 percent by 1978.

The U.S. has been gobbling up oil. Just from the point of view of oil, it is easy to see why German and Swiss currency in the past skyrocketed in value in relation to the U.S. dollar.

Monetary results of increased oil consumption

Let's consider the problem the U.S. has brought upon itself by its increased consumption of oil. If we take the largest Arab oil producer, Saudi Arabia, we find that oil payments go something like this. The U.S. buys oil from Saudi Arabia and pays for it in U.S. dollars. The currency in Saudi Arabia is the riyal. (The exchange rate as of this writing is about 3.2 riyals to the dollar. In 1971 it was about 4.2 to 1.) Normally, we would expect that Saudi Arabia would convert dollars into riyals. The Arab country is small, however (in terms of population), with a comparatively small money supply. To exchange dollars for riyals would quickly drive up the price of riyals, affecting the marketing of oil.

To get around this problem, Saudi Arabia does not convert all the dollars it receives into riyals. Rather, it temporarily holds some as dollar deposits in banks. Then, when the Saudis wish to purchase something from the U.S. or make an investment in America, they use these U.S. dollars. In theory this method should result in nearly all the dollars we pay the Saudis returning to the U.S. in the form of purchases of American exports and Saudi investment.

Unfortunately, this is not the case. For one thing, the Saudis can frequently buy competing products cheaper in Germany or Japan (because of greater productivity, lower inflation, etc., in those countries). For another, the Saudis often buy products from other nations simply because those nations produce items that we don't offer. Finally, our inflation rate directly affects the Saudis' wealth because they are using our currency. Consequently, to avoid a dollar loss in value because of inflation, it is to their advantage to convert any extra dollars (those not currently in use for investment or commodity purchases) into gold, Swiss francs, German marks, Japanese yen, etc., and then hold that money in those other currencies.

The net result of all these factors is that we are not receiving back nearly as many dollars as we are giving to the Saudis in exchange for oil. (And the Saudis are unhappy because the dollars we give them are worth less in buying power because of our inflation.) This dollar glut, as we've already seen, has resulted in a lowering of the U.S. dollar in value in relation to the currency of stronger currency nations.

This is why the U.S. dollar fell dramatically in relation to the German mark, Swiss franc, and Japanese yen, and not so dramatically against other currencies.

How could the U.S. get those oil dollars back and relieve the downward currency pressure on the dollar? One method I have heard frequently suggested is to increase the cost of food that we export. Since we are still the world's largest food exporter, by dramatically increasing the price of food, in theory we should immediately begin getting more dollars back. "Let the oil-producers eat sand if they want to charge so much for oil," is an expression I have heard more than once.

Unfortunately, things rarely work out simplistically. Were the U.S. to raise the price of food to even ten times its present cost, the oil producers would not starve. Remember, they have the enormous wealth from their oil and could easily pay the price. And, if the price got ridiculously high, they could always raise the price of oil correspondingly high. Rather, raising the price of food would mean that poor, underdeveloped countries, which buy a large portion of the food, would no longer be able to afford it. These countries would have no recourse and their populations would starve.

This also would result in a great decrease in the quantity of food exported. (See demand/supply explanation in Chapter 2.) The net effect of fewer sales at higher prices could actually result in fewer dollars coming back to the U.S. than increased sales at lower prices! Food is not an economic weapon for the United States.

In response to this argument I have heard some urge that we only sell high-priced food in the Middle East or otherwise restrict the food that goes to that area alone unless oil prices go down. Food, however, is a commodity. It goes to the highest bidder. Those with money never starve because they can always buy food from others if they are willing to pay enough. I repeat, food is not an economic weapon.

This hostile response by some in the U.S. is simply a misunderstanding of the situation. We can easily bring the price of oil down by cutting our consumption (demand) of the product. Barring that, we must increase export items to OPEC and encourage their investment here in order to balance dollars sent there.

(It's interesting to consider the possibilities of serious OPEC investment in the U.S. given the enormous quantities of money involved. I have heard an educated guess that it would take only 50 years for the OPEC countries to own this country if they devoted their energies primarily toward investing in the U.S. It seems that even encouraging foreign investment domestically as a way to recoup domestic currency has its limits. What it does is pass ownership of one country's wealth to another. The oil-producing nations, however, seem to be far more interested in buying expensive consumer products and guns than they are in investing here. Each year they spend as much and sometimes more than their income on such items.)

In 1979 the Iranian revolution again caused a worldwide shortage of oil supplies. (Iran was formerly the world's second largest exporter.) The oil-producing nations used this shortage, temporary though it may have been, to substantially increase oil prices. What resulted from this action?

An increase in oil prices results in increased cost of all petroleum-related products. For industrial nations that use great quantities of imported oil this is reflected in an increased rate of price inflation. Nations which import great quantities of oil include Germany, Switzerland, Japan, and the United States. (England, because of its North Sea oil, is relatively unaffected.) The higher inflation rate caused by substantially increased oil prices has an adverse effect on the currencies of these countries. The value of their currencies is likely to fall relative to the value of currencies in countries that are not so dependent on imported oil. This accounts for the surge in value of the British pound (North Sea oil) and the dramatic drop in the yen (no domestic Japanese oil) in early 1979.

What are the effects on the U.S. of the oil price increase? Since the U.S. imports about half its oil, our inflation rate is also affected, however, not to the degree that those countries which import all their oil are affected.

An interesting sidelight is to speculate on what the world's largest oil producer, the Saudis, might do if they eventually get entirely fed up with the weakness of the dollar. One possibility is to print billions of riyals and then tie them to oil in a fashion similar to the way the U.S. once tied the dollar to gold. One riyal, for example, might be worth one barrel (or one gallon) of oil. Instantly the riyal would become the world's strongest and most desired currency and quickly would supersede the dollar.

This would make the Saudis the world's bankers and relegate the U.S. to the position of a "second class" nation. (In the short run, of course, this might backfire. Without being able to pay in dollars, the U.S. might be forced to cut back oil imports, thereby driving down the value of oil.)

7

Anticipating trends

WE HAVE EXAMINED many reasons for the dollar's drop in value in the recent past. However, the path of the dollar has not been a straight line downward. Rather, if you'll recall Chart 5B, it has been an up and down line. Although in the long run between 1975 and 1978 the course was downward, at any given moment it could have been either a short burst up or a short burst down. (This concept is critical to understanding successful money futures investments discussed in Chapter 10.)

CHART 7A Graphic appearance of currency trends

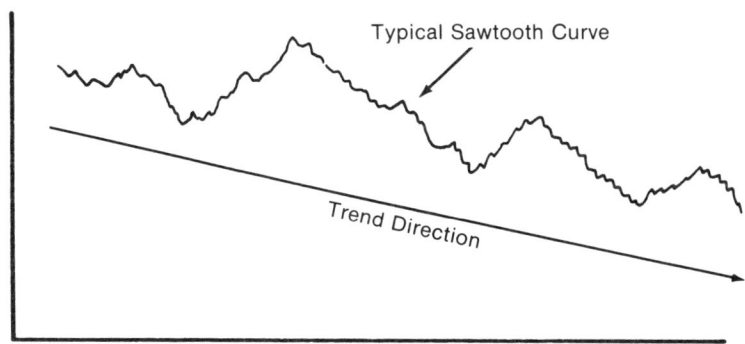

Why does the dollar not simply fall, if the trend is downward, in a straight line? The answer is the same as for any market. There are forces at work which increase the dollar's value. And there are forces at work which pressure it down. In the long run the stronger force wins. But, in the short run, the weaker force can win many small battles. For example, in the period we are discussing, central banks were the weaker force. Quite often they could succeed, temporarily, in stabilizing the dollar or even getting it to bounce back a bit. But, the economic forces we have been discussing were stronger and they always came back more powerful to tear the dollar down.

It is valuable to understand the timing of these ups and downs.

The currency markets (including gold) tend to be volatile. By that I mean that they respond emotionally to news, good or bad. For example, let's first consider some bad news.

On the weekend of December 16-17, 1978, the OPEC countries (after determining the war in Iran had severely cut back supplies) announced a 14 percent increase in the price of oil during 1979. The next few days the American dollar plunged as much as 2 percent in relation to other currencies. Why? Did the OPEC announcement immediately result in more dollars going out of the U.S. to the oil-producing nations, thereby depressing the dollar's value?

Hardly. The announcement was for a price increase that would not take place until the next year and then in small increments. At the time the dollar fell in value there was absolutely no real effect caused by the price increase.

Why, then, did the dollar fall on the announcement? The answer is anticipation. Those who deal in currency immediately saw the eventual effect of the price increase. It meant that sometime during the following year the number of dollars going for oil would increase and since at that time the prospects for more dollars coming back was remote, it appeared that a dollar value plunge was going to come. Those in the know (and there are many, including private individuals and bankers) bailed out of dollars. The price fell.

Now, let's consider the opposite case. Suppose that the United States announces a contract to export huge quantities of war materials to the OPEC nations, a contract worth tens of billions of dollars over a few months' period. In this case, we could expect the dollar to firm and even rise. And, this would happen as soon as the announcement was made, long before the effect of dollars coming back from exports really occurred.

Therefore, we may conclude that economic announcements will drive the dollar up or down depending on their nature. But, we need a bit of refinement. Rarely do announcements come unannounced. In our first example, the world knew for perhaps six months or longer that the OPEC countries would meet and would raise the price of oil. The announcement should have come as no surprise. (And similarly, defense agreements often must go through Congress, and their eventual announcement also is rarely a surprise.) The announcement itself should have been anticipated and investors should much earlier have adjusted their money positions. Why, then, did the actual announcement produce a big currency result?

Although an announcement could be anticipated, the exact nature of the announcement could not. Concerning the oil increase, the best judgment before was that an 8 percent price increase could be expected. Should that have been the actual announcement, chances are the currency market would have not moved significantly in response. On the other hand, if the announcement had been a decision not to raise prices at all, the market undoubtedly would have driven the dollar higher because it would come as a surprise and most investors again would not yet have adjusted their positions. When the 14 percent increase was announced, it too was a surprise—so investors moved swiftly to adjust.

A gambler betting on a higher than expected increase in the price of oil could have made a bundle by buying strong currencies the Friday before the increase. Of course, a gambler betting no increase and buying dollars (selling foreign currencies) could have lost just as much.

92 Buying and selling currency for profit

The market for currency moves up and down in the *very short run* largely because of surprise and anticipation of economic and political news (and by central bank intervention). These adjustments are what account for the sawtooth look of currency value curves. There remains an additional question. According to everything we've discussed—the economic factors and the emotion of the market between 1974 and 1978—the value of U.S. dollars in relation to other currencies should have a curve looking roughly like the one drawn on Chart 7B. The actual curve, however, looks like the one drawn on Chart 7C.

CHART 7B Expected United States dollar foreign currency value

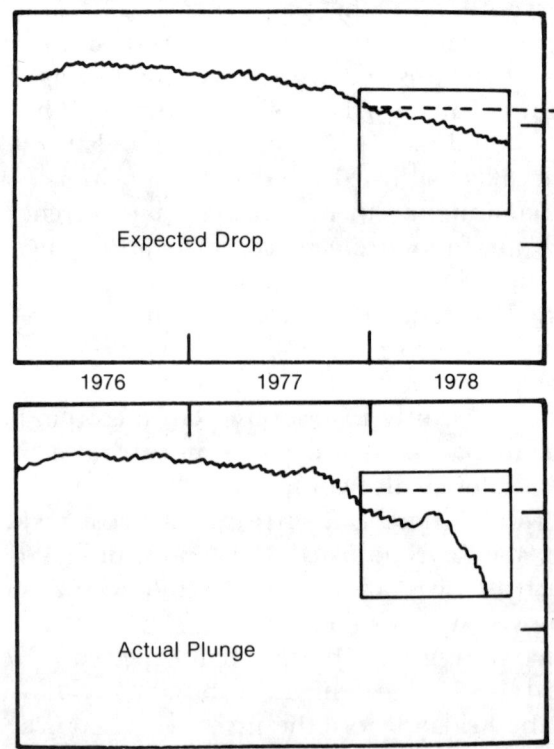

CHART 7C Actual United States dollar foreign currency value

What we're concerned with is the dramatic plunge that took place in 1978. It allowed investors in currency to make fortunes by selling dollars and buying other currencies. Why did the dollar *suddenly* drop?

To the best of my knowledge, all the factors influencing the declining dollar worked gradually. There was no single announcement, no sudden change in an economic indicator that should have pushed the dollar over the edge of a cliff. Yet, the dollar did fall over a cliff. I have heard some eminent financiers speculate that if the U.S. government had not, for the first time in recent history, intervened, the dollar plunge would not have stopped on its own. It would have fallen indefinitely, pulling the U.S. economy and the rest of the world into an enormous depression that would make the 1929 crash and depression of the '30s look like child's play.

Equally important: Is the force that pushed the dollar off the cliff still in existence today, ready to strike again (and to afford profits to those who have placed themselves in a position to take advantage)?

I believe the answer is yes. The force is the so-called and much misunderstood Euro-dollar.

8

The Eurodollar trap

WHY DID THE U.S. DOLLAR fall so far so fast in 1978? Is such a plunge likely to happen again?

In this chapter we are not so much concerned with what caused the fall of the dollar as with the size of that fall. The explanation of the size of the fall is something the popular press has dubbed the "Eurodollar."

I have listened to some monetary writers scoff at the Eurodollar. I have heard it said that the Eurodollar has no real significance because it is borrowed money, money that is not available for spending, and consequently, could not contribute to the drop in value of U.S. dollars. Nothing could be further from the truth. The Eurodollar is what caused the magnitude of the loss in value of U.S. dollars in 1978. And should another decline in the U.S. dollar begin, the Eurodollar could again accelerate its size.

What, then, is the "Eurodollar?"

The Eurodollar is quite simply U.S. dollars located in

Europe. We might speak just as glibly of South American dollars or Los Angeles dollars or New York dollars. It is the geographic location of the dollars that gives them their name. They are still U.S. dollars.

In order to understand the influence of Europe-located dollars we must first understand a little about banking and the creation of money.

Money

Just as in the primitive village we discussed in Chapter 2, our society today relies in large part on coins and currency for money. As of this writing there is a little over 112 billion dollars of coin and currency in circulation.

It is important to understand that this is "fiat" money. It has no intrinsic value (such as gold or silver may have) but its value, rather, is stipulated by the federal government. We accept it because we know that others in turn will accept it from us. I am still amazed when I go into a bank and ask the teller for dollar coins. He or she invariably asks, "Oh, you want silver dollars?" Indeed, I would love to get silver dollars in change. But, the bank won't give them to me, at least not for 100 cents. The price of a real silver dollar with no collector value is about $10–20 U.S. That's the value of the silver in it. Since 1964 the U.S. has not issued any silver coinage for circulation. (The government has issued many part-silver coins intended strictly for collectors and sold at a higher cost.)

In our primitive village we saw that the man who owned the gold mine issued gold coins. He had to work hard to extract the metal from the earth and then coined it. But when he issued paper money, his hard-working days were over. The same is true for the government. When there was silver in our coins, the government had to pay for that silver. Eventually, the government was paying close to a dollar just for the silver in the dollar coin. It was at this point that the fiat money was issued.

Today's dollar is the Susan B. Anthony "mini-coin." It is made of cupro-nickel—a clad or "sandwich" coin of two non-precious metals. The best estimate of the U.S. mint is that it costs about three cents to make each coin including the cost of the metal, its preparation, minting, and all other charges. That means that on each coin released to circulation, the government makes a profit of 97 cents. That profit is technically called the government's seignorage.

Paper money is also fiat and the Bureau of Engraving and Printing, which prints all our money, indicates that it costs not much more to print a $20 bill than to strike the $1 coin. That means that for every $20 bill issued, the government's seignorage is roughly $19.97.

Of course, all currency and coinage issued isn't new. Much of it goes to replace worn-out money that is withdrawn from circulation. But, more money is created in this fashion each year than is destroyed. In fact, each year the increase in the total amount of currency and coinage is greater than the year before. (What does this indicate about inflation?) Chart 8A is a graph of this supply of money.

CHART 8A Supply of currency and coin

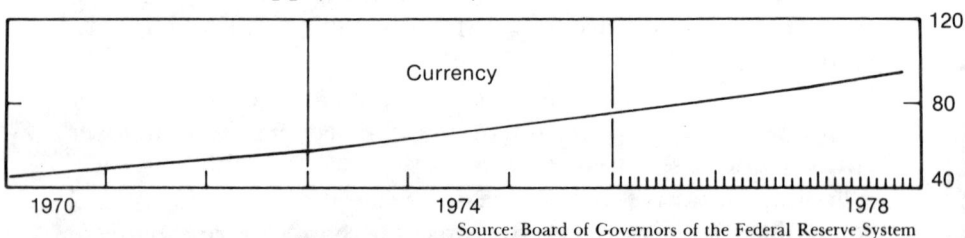

Source: Board of Governors of the Federal Reserve System

What does the government do with the seignorage it acquires? It goes to the treasury and is used to pay government expenses including the huge national debt. We'll come back to the national debt in a little while, but now let's follow that fiat currency that the government has created.

In our primitive village there was only coin and paper money. Our society is far more sophisticated. We have banks and checking accounts. If we deposit $100 cash into a bank checking account, then although we don't have that money any longer in the form of currency and coin with us personally, we can still get it back any time we demand it simply by writing a check. (Which is why it's called a "demand" account.) Some might argue that there's little difference between a checking account and cash—$100 when you want it is still $100.

True, however, when we are allowed to write checks an interesting thing happens. We end up with more than the cash and currency we started with. In fact, at the present time the total in demand (checking) accounts (not including coins and currency) is almost 270 billion dollars. Since we've just said that a check for most practical purposes is as good as cash, when we add currency and coin and demand deposit balances together we find that the total amount of money in circulation in the U.S. is more than 360 billion dollars! Of this amount only about 30 percent is in the form of currency and coins. This measurement of the money supply is called "M-1" stock.

Our financial institutions, however, are not limited to simply holding checking accounts. They can also hold savings accounts. The next time you open a bank savings account, take a close look at the brochure that comes with the passbook describing the account. Typically it will say that withdrawals can be made only upon giving the bank 30 days advance notice. Of course, the bank has the right to waive the 30-day-notice requirement and normally does. But, that 30-day notice means that in theory you cannot get your money out upon demand as you can with a checking account. You must wait a certain time period first. Consequently, these deposits are called "time deposits." At present U.S. banks hold some 600 billion dollars in time deposits.

Now, while a time deposit isn't exactly like cash in the way checks, coins, and currency are, it's very similar. After all, 30 days isn't all that long to wait to get the cash. Consequently, if we add the time deposits to the demand deposits, coins, and

Buying and selling currency for profit

currency, we find that the total amount of money in circulation is close to 1,000 billion dollars. This is usually called the "M-2" measurement of money.

There are yet other sources of "cash." There are the savings (time) deposits at mutual savings banks, at savings and loan associations, and at credit unions. When these are added in the total, supply of money jumps to over 1,500 billion (1.5 trillion) dollars. This is termed the "M-3" measurement. Chart 8B shows the growth of the money supply for M1, 2, and 3 over the last 70 years in the United States.

Now we're talking about a total money supply (M-3) of 1,500 billion dollars. Yet, you'll recall that we stated the total of currency and coins in circulation was only about 112 billion. If that's the case then there's actually 150 times more total money in circulation than there is cash and currency. (Please note that unlike our medieval example, these figures are not hypothetical. They are supplied to the public by the Federal Reserve Bank. The method of calculating M-1, M-2, and M-3 was changed in 1980, but is still similar to the one described here.) Where did the extra money come from?

Financing the national debt

Some of it was created by the U.S. government in an attempt to finance the national debt. Almost every year over the past four decades the government has spent more money on defense, education, welfare, and so on, than it has taken in through taxes. If you or I were to spend more than we earned each year, we'd quickly be forced into bankruptcy. But, the federal government has a clever way of handling its overexpenditure which keeps it going indefinitely—it monetizes the national debt. (Note: There is nothing wrong with having a national debt; it is essential, according to modern economic concepts, to have a debt in order to have prosperous times. Having an excessive debt is the problem.)

When the debt exceeds taxes, the Treasury resorts to borrow-

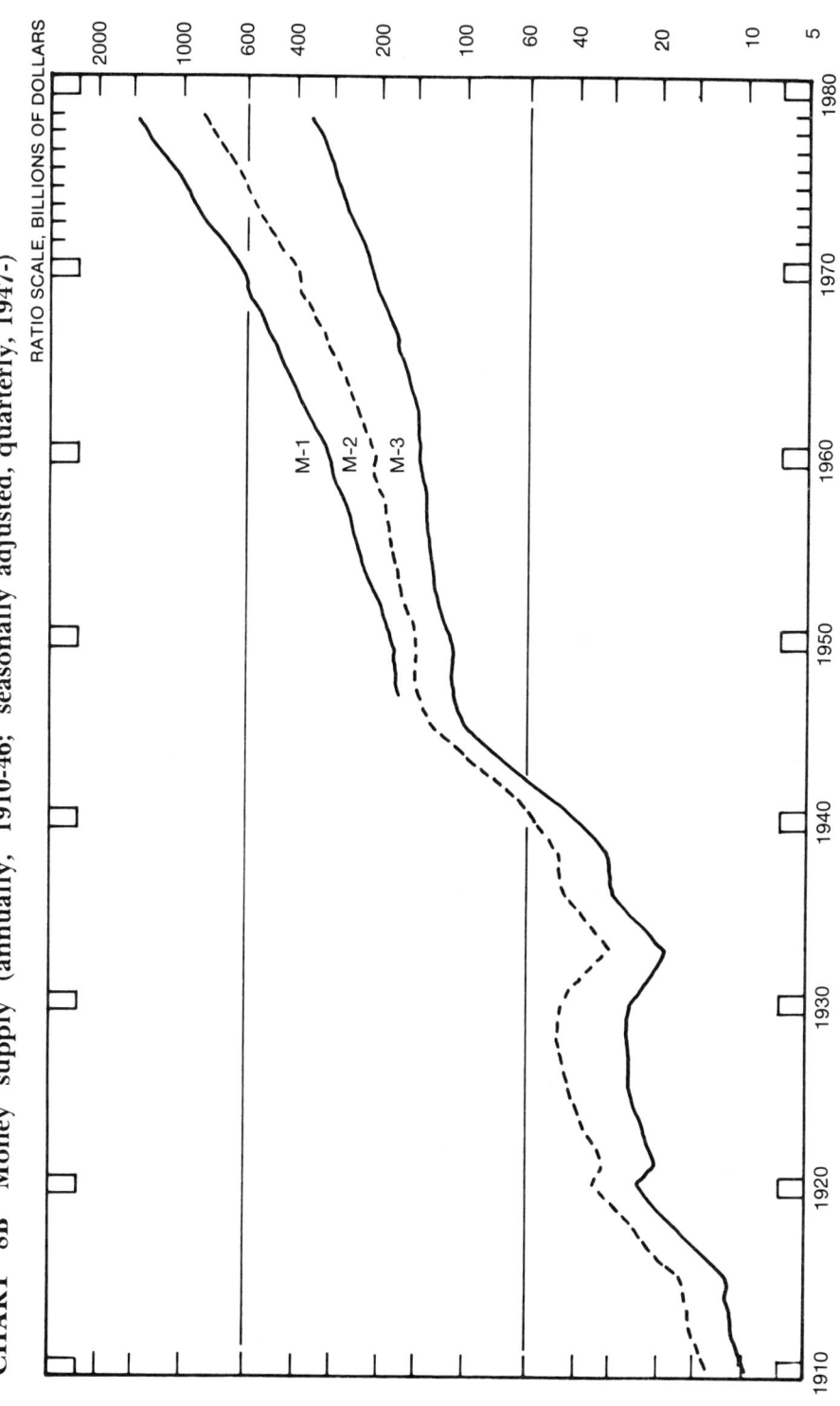

CHART 8B Money supply (annually, 1910-46; seasonally adjusted, quarterly, 1947-)

ing. The Treasury issues "bonds." These are often large denomination borrowings and are purchased largely by the Federal Reserve. (Financial institutions including banks, insurance companies, and many well-off individuals also are purchasers.) The Treasury then uses the money it receives to pay the government's bills. It also, of course, pays interest on this borrowed money.

At this point some readers unfamiliar with government financing may perceive a problem. The point of the bonds is to borrow money to help pay for the national debt. Yet, the Federal Reserve, a big purchaser, is another government agency. How, therefore, can one government agency's (Treasury) borrowing from another government agency (Federal Reserve) yield additional money to the government? If my left pocket lends my right pocket a dollar, do I have more total money? Yes, if I happen to be the government.

When the Federal Reserve purchases government bonds, it does so in part by issuing Federal Reserve notes based on deposits made by member banks. It creates new money. (This will be explained in detail with examples from the private sector.) It uses the new money to service the national debt. The new money is the "federal reserve."

Many people are concerned about the size of the national debt. They refer to it as an "overhang" or a "burden" or even a "time bomb." Because it is necessary each year not only to finance the deficit, but also to pay the interest on deficits that were previously financed, it appears that eventually the national debt will consume all of our money.

This simply will not wash. Much of the finance charge (interest) ends up back in the Treasury. (The Federal Reserve receives interest on its purchased Treasury borrowings, which it deposits back in the Treasury!) Secondly, although our national debt has been growing at an enormous rate, so has our GNP. When the national debt is considered as a percentage of real Gross National Product, we find that it is not at all alarming (see Chart 8D).

CHART 8C Net federal debt (amount outstanding; end of year, 1946-51; seasonally adjusted, end of quarter, 1952-)

CHART 8D Federal debt expressed as a percent of Gross National Product (GNP)

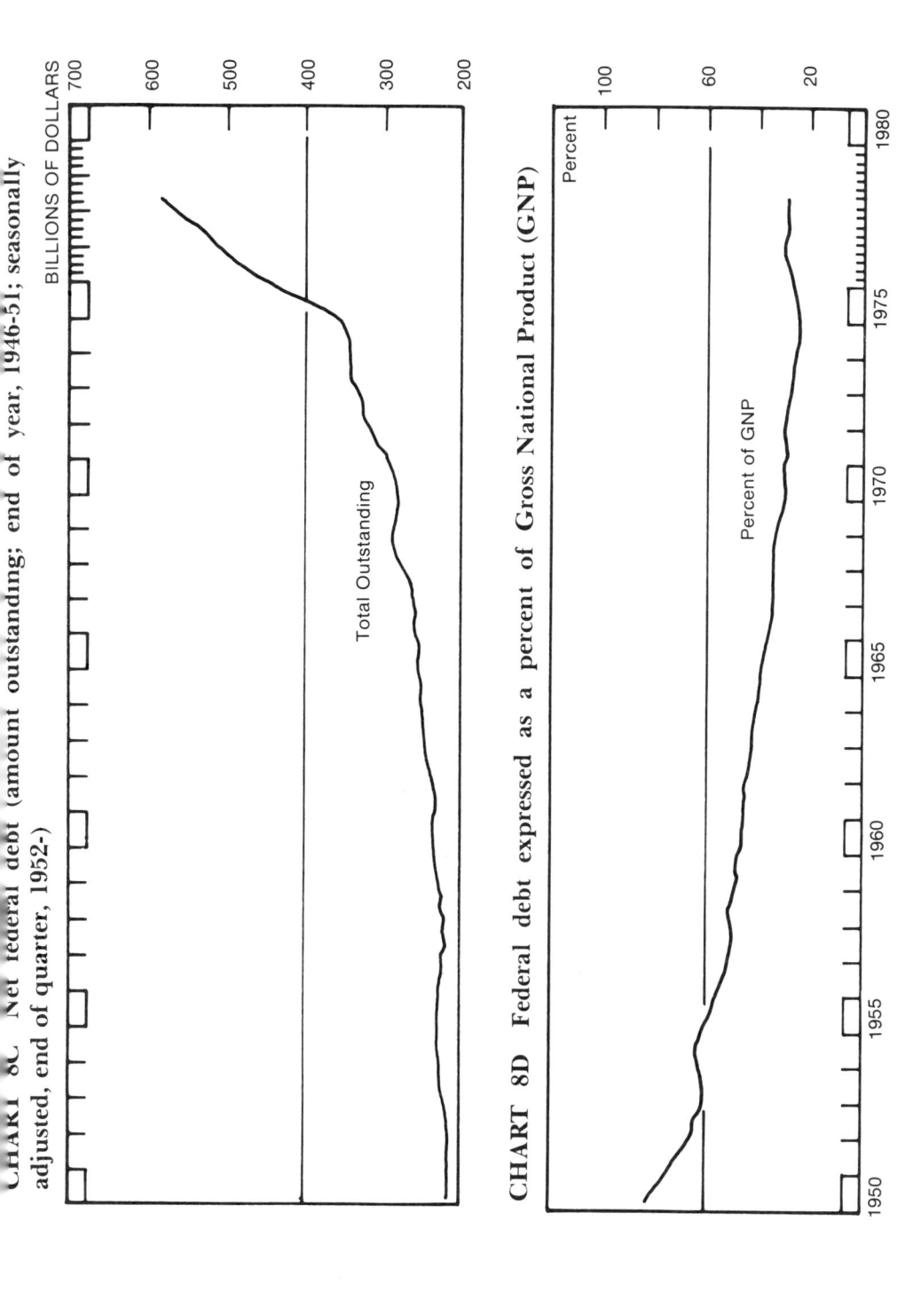

To summarize, we've seen that the basic source of new money in the country is the government. We've also seen what money is (coins, currency, demand and time deposits), and we've seen why the government creates more of it all the time (national debt). Now, let's look at an entirely different source of new money.

Banking

When a bank is opened, the goal of the owners is not usually altruistic—it's profit oriented. Perhaps the owners have a million dollars in capital. They invest their million dollars in a bank in the same way that other people invest money in a fast-food franchise or in chicken ranches—to make more money. But how does a bank, in fact, make money?

There are a number of ways, but the primary way is by lending money. To see how this is done, let's consider the case of Rita's bank.

Rita has a million dollars in cash and she gains a bank charter. Rita knows that to succeed she must attract customers, so the first thing she does is build a huge bank building with marble columns and solid brass doors. This costs her $500,000. She now begins a set of books. This is a necessity also for several reasons: She will want to know how her own money is doing; her customers will want to know how their money is doing; and the IRS will want to know how everyone's money is doing.

Rita uses a double-entry bookkeeping system. This is standard accounting procedure. It accounts for all money by indicating where it came from and where it went to. It shows all money as both an asset and a liability. Rita's books look like this:

Bank of Rita

Assets		Liabilities	
cash	$500,000	capital	$1,000,000
building	$500,000		

Now Rita is ready for business and she opens her doors with a big sign stating that she will pay interest on time (savings) deposits and will offer demand deposits (checking accounts) for only a two-dollar-a-month service charge.

Almost immediately she has a customer. David has just sold a patent to a government agency. He has a check from the Treasury for half a million dollars. He deposits $250,000 in a savings (time) account and $250,000 in a demand (checking) account. Now Rita's books look like this:

Bank of Rita

Assets		Liabilities	
cash	$1,000,000	capital	$1,000,000
building	500,000	demand deposit (David)	250,000
		time deposit (David)	250,000

Notice in the bookkeeping system used that the $500,000 shows up twice. On the liability side it shows up as a deposit—it's a liability because it's money the bank owes to David. On the asset side it shows up as additional cash, because that's what David deposited into the bank.

Rita has joined the Federal Reserve System. (Roughly half the banks in the country representing 75 percent of the money belong to the Federal Reserve System.) In order to facilitate the cashing of checks with other banks and in order to meet government requirements, the Federal Reserve requires that each member bank keep on deposit with the "Fed" a certain portion of each customer's deposit. Let's say that at this time the amount required is 20 percent of all demand accounts and 5 percent of all time accounts. That means that Rita must now deposit 20 percent of David's demand account and 5 percent of his time account with the Federal Reserve; Rita must deposit $62,500. She does this and the new entry on her books simply shifts the money from cash to the Federal Reserve.

Bank of Rita

Assets		Liabilities	
cash	$937,500	capital	$1,000,000
building	500,000	demand deposit (David)	250,000
Fed. Reserve	62,500	time deposit (David)	250,000

Thus far, Rita has spent a considerable amount of money (on a building), has accepted money on which she's agreed to pay interest (David's time deposit), and has agreed to handle his checking account for a nominal fee. On the surface it would seem she is not a particularly good business person since all her effort shows as expenses and none as income. [Note, federal law precludes Rita from considering David's deposit money as income (profit) to herself.]

Creating "private" money

How does she go about earning money? Most banks would do this in several ways. One way is by buying government securities (Treasury bonds) which would pay interest. Presumably the interest paid to the bank would be higher than the interest the bank would pay to David, leaving a difference as the bank's own income.

For our example, however, we'll assume that Rita bypasses buying government securities and instead offers to make loans. It just so happens that Morgan Le Grand is getting ready to build a shopping center and he needs to borrow $900,000 to complete the project. Rita lends him that amount of money. This leaves her with $37,500, more than enough to meet any expected cash demands of David (who, after all, could conceivably write a check for $25,000, bring it in, and demand that it be changed into currency.)

Note that lending the money out did not in any way affect the liability side of Rita's books. It simply transferred money

Bank of Rita

Assets		Liabilities	
cash	$37,500	capital	$1,000,000
building	500,000	demand deposit (David)	250,000
Fed. Reserve	62,500	time deposit (David)	250,000
loan (Morgan)	900,000		

from the cash account on the asset side to the loan account on the asset side. (Since the money is in the form of an I.O.U. to Rita from Morgan, it is considered an asset by Rita. Morgan, of course, would consider it a debt or liability on his books.)

What does Morgan do with the money? He doesn't need it immediately, since it will be some time before he has to pay his laborers and material suppliers, so he deposits it in his own bank in a demand account (no interest paid to him, but he gets the money whenever he wants it). Morgan's bank is the Boomerang Trust Co. It receives the deposit from Morgan for $900,000 and opens a demand (checking) account for him. Then it calls upon the Bank of Rita for the $900,000.

(In actual practice, the Boomerang Trust Co. could open a demand deposit of its own in Rita's bank or her bank could deposit the $900,000 with the Federal Reserve and Boomerang Trust could have that amount transferred to its own account at the Fed. No cash in the form of coin or currency changes hands.)

In any event, Boomerang's own books now show this addition:

Boomerang Trust Co.

Assets		Liabilities	
cash	$900,000	demand deposit (Morgan Le Grand)	$900,000

Of course Boomerang is in business to make money also, so it immediately makes plans to lend out its new assets (reserves). It must first, of course, put an appropriate amount of it ($180,000) in the Federal Reserve. This leaves it $720,000 to lend out, which it does to Lillian who is borrowing the money to refurbish her new Beverly Hills guesthouse.

Lillian has just opened an account at Rita's bank, so she deposits the money there. (And Rita either has the money transferred to her account from Boomerang Trust at the Federal Reserve or opens her own demand account at Boomerang. No coins or currency have changed hands.)

Lillian puts the money in a time account, since she doesn't know when exactly she'll need the money. A time account requires a 5 percent reserve so Rita deposits $36,000 in the Federal Reserve and now has $684,000 additional reserves to lend out.

Bank of Rita

Assets		Liabilities	
cash	$37,500	capital	$1,000,000
building	500,000	demand deposit (David)	250,000
Fed. Reserve	98,500	time deposit (David)	250,000
loan	900,000	time deposit (Lillian)	720,000
reserve available for lending	684,000		

At the end of this cycle, assuming Rita makes the loan of $684,000, she will have lent out a total of $1,584,000—or $84,000 more than the total capital and cash deposited in her bank ($584,000 more than the cash she started with)! In addition, Boomerang Trust will have lent out $720,000 for a grand total of $2,304,000. This does not include the reserves that each bank still maintains at the Federal Reserve (Rita's bank—$98,500; Boomerang—$180,000). And the chain of lending has not ended. The $684,000 will eventually be deposited in some other bank which will lend it out again.

The total number of times that the same money can be lent depends on several factors. If there were no reserve requirements whatever and no leakage (which we'll explain shortly), theoretically a deposit of only $100 could be lent out over and over again, eventually resulting in an infinite amount of money. If the reserve requirements were 10 percent, and there was no leakage, then $100 could be lent out enough times to create $1,000.

	Deposit	Reserve	Loaned
	$100	$10	$90
	90	9	81
	81	8.10	72.9
	72.9	7.29	65.61
	65.61	———	———
	———	———	———
Totals:	1,000	100	1,000

Of course, our example did not take into account that not everyone immediately deposits money taken out in a loan. Some of it is held in the form of currency for a period of time. This is "leakage," which further restricts the amount of money that can be generated by banks.

Several things should be obvious from this example. First, banks create money. Second, if you asked any individual banker (Rita or Boomerang) if they had created money, they would very likely say no. Rita would say simply that she lent out money that had been deposited in her bank, first by David, later by Lillian. Boomerang would say that it merely lent out money that Morgan had deposited. Each bank taken alone did not create money. But the banking system all together had created an enormous amount of money. It is largely because of this entire process of monetizing the debt and fractional reserve banking that we can have less than 112 billion dollars in currency and coins and over 1,500 billion dollars in total money supply.

Federal reserve controls

We'll apply this process to the Eurodollar in just a moment, but before we do, consider one last aspect of fractional reserve banking—the reserve. When you deposit any money in a demand account (or even a time account for that matter) what you really want is liquidity. Liquidity is another word for cash. You want to be able to demand and receive from the bank at any time of the day or night the cash back that you stuck in. Of course, because you are receiving interest on a time account, you give up some of your demands and agree to a waiting period; and because you can't find a bank open at two a.m., you give up some of your requirements on the demand account. (Note, recently banks have been blending time and demand accounts allowing immediate transfers from savings to checking. If anything, this only creates additional money supplies.)

How does a bank provide liquidity? Ideally it does so by taking your cash deposit and storing it (in the form of gold or some other valued commodity including silver coins) so that when you demand it back, it's instantly there. A truly liquid bank (of which there are some in Europe) maintains reserves of at least 100 percent.

A typical U.S. bank, however, usually has only a few percent of its deposit liabilities available in cash. There's some currency in the vault, coins in the drawers, and deposits at the Federal Reserve, but that's about all. It is not liquid—rather, it has loaned out its reserves in order to increase its profits from interest on the loans. If we assume an average of 15 percent reserves in the Federal Reserve and another 5 pecent in cash (a high figure) a typical bank really only may have 20 percent of its liability in reserves at any given time. If there should be a run on the bank and depositors holding more than 20 percent of funds demand cash, the bank might not immediately be able to meet its responsibilities. Of course, that's why there is a time period on savings accounts, to allow the bank to liquidate other assets. And the Federal Deposit Insurance Corporation also would step in to guarantee many accounts up to its maximum limit. As long as a demand for cash occurred only at a single bank, even a large one, there would be enough resources available during most periods of economic health to easily weather the storm. Of course, if times were bad and banks could not readily liquidate their assets (call in or sell loans) and there was a simultaneous run on all banks, the financial institutions and the government would be hard pressed.

Nobody really expects that to happen, however; otherwise, who would put money in a non-liquid bank?

The point to note here is that the function of the reserve that banks keep at the Federal Reserve (there are 12 Fed banks around the country) is not primarily to protect the bank against runs or failure—confidence in the banking system by the general public does that—rather it is to *control the amount by which banks can create more money*. Remember, we said that if no reserves were required (and there was no leakage) the amount of money created would be unlimited. The greater the reserve requirements, the smaller the amount of new money that can be created by banks. The more liquid the Federal Reserve requires banks to be, the less money they can create.

This is the ultimate tool of the Federal Reserve for controlling the money supply created by the banks. Historically, however, the Federal Reserve has chosen to use this tool very rarely. When the Federal Reserve was started, the original reserve requirement was only 3 percent. Recently it has been around 18 percent for demand deposits and 5 percent for time deposits (large metropolitan banks). In between, it's been adjusted very few times with only about a score of moves in

110   Buying and selling currency for profit

the last quarter century. Rather, the Fed has chosen to adjust the discount rate. This is the charge it makes to member banks for borrowing money from the Federal Reserve.

Therefore, although the United States has a fractional banking system, that system is closely and strictly controlled by the Federal Reserve. It limits the amount of new money that banks can create through lending of their deposits.

The Eurodollar system

Consider the case of Harvey. Harvey dealt in diamonds around the world. On one of his many trips he sold some diamonds in the U.S. to a customer who paid him one million dollars for them. Harvey deposited his money in the LFB (Looking For Business) Bank in Chicago. The million dollars was used by the LFB Bank of Chicago to create loans in the usual way we have discussed. Harvey was an international traveler, however, and soon he departed the U.S. for England. Wanting his money nearby, he wrote a check on the Chicago bank and opened a demand (checking account) deposit in London in the CLEB (Cockney Looking For Business) Bank. Now let's consider what happened in this exchange of money between banks.

The London bank, being foreign, did not belong to the U.S. Federal Reserve System; consequently, it could not have its account at the Fed credited with the million and the Chicago bank's account debited. So, instead it opened its own demand account with the Chicago bank and deposited one million dollars (Harvey's money).

From the Chicago bank's point of view, nothing much had happened. Harvey had withdrawn one million; the London bank had deposited one million. The liabilities remained the same (although with different names on the accounts).

For the London bank, however, something different had occurred. Its assets and liabilities sheet were now increased by one million dollars.

CLFB Bank—London

Assets	Liabilities
$1,000,000	$1,000,000 (Harvey)

Note that the account in the Chicago bank which Harvey deposited from the diamond sale was in dollars. The account in the London bank was also in dollars, and the demand deposit of the London bank on the Chicago bank also was in dollars. No conversion to foreign currency was made. However, the dollars located in the Chicago bank were American-dollars; those in the London bank were Eurodollars. (Remember, it's where they are that determines what they're called. If the deposit were in Hong Kong they would be Asian dollars. In Sao Paulo they would be South American dollars . . . and so forth.)

Now, the London bank proceeded to do what any good American bank would do: It prepared to lend the money out. It looked around to see if there was anyone who wanted to borrow American dollars. As it turned out, there was a French bassoon company with an English branch office that was planning to buy a computer from an American company. It would, of course, have to pay for the computer in dollars, since the company selling was American, so it borrowed money from the London bank. As it turned out, the London bank was a non-liquid bank which felt it only needed to keep 10 percent in reserves. (Deposits in *U.S. Dollar accounts* were little regulated by the English government.) It held onto $100,000 and lent the French bassoon company $900,000, which they in turn paid to the French branch of the American computer company. The French branch of the American computer company deposited the $900,000 in a French bank, the W&DLFB (Wine And Dine Looking For Business) Bank of Paris.

The London bank withdrew $900,000 U.S. of its demand

deposit in the Chicago bank; this was the loan which the bassoon company gave to the computer company, which deposited it in the Paris bank. Since it was a dollar denominated deposit, the Paris bank immediately opened up a demand deposit in an American bank. Just by coincidence it happened to be the LFB Bank of Chicago.

What's happened from the Chicago bank's point of view? Very little:

LFB Bank of Chicago

Assets		Liabilities	
cash	$1,000,000	demand deposit London	$100,000
		demand deposit Paris	900,000

The Chicago bank still had only one million dollars in demand deposits. Of course, the names have been switched around. First it was Harvey; now it's partly to the London bank and partly to the Paris bank. But the total demand deposits remain at one million.

The Paris bank, however, has a totally new deposit in the form of $900,000 U.S. And what do you suppose the Paris bank will do with that money?

As it turns out, the Paris bank believes in holding only 5 percent reserves. It pays a higher rate of interest on all deposits in order to attract business in spite of the "added risk." Also, it too does not belong to the U.S. "Fed" nor is it much regulated on U.S. dollar deposits. Consequently, the French bank now has $855,000 to lend out, which it does to a German company buying chocolate from a Swiss company which wants to receive payment in dollars for other business reasons.

The Swiss chocolate company plays one more round in the banking circle. It deposits its money in a dollar denominated account in a Swiss bank, the CLFB (Chocolate Looking For Business) Bank of Zurich. The bank of Paris demands

$855,000 of its deposit in the Chicago bank and turns it over to the Swiss bank. The Swiss bank opens a demand deposit in, that's correct, the LFB Bank of Chicago.* Have there been any changes in the Chicago bank's books? Only in the names on the deposits.

LFB Bank of Chicago

Assets		Liabilities	
cash	$1,000,000	demand deposit London	$100,000
		demand deposit Paris	45,000
		demand deposit Zurich	855,000
		Total	$1,000,000

Of course, the Zurich bank feels $855,000 richer, and since it is a totally non-liquid bank (has no reserves at all) feels perfectly confident in lending out the entire amount!

Note: European banks seem to determine their reserve requirements on the basis of how much cash they might have to come up with at any given moment in order to meet withdrawals. Depending on the type of loans made, and time deposits received, it is far from inconceivable for such a bank to feel that no cash reserves are required.

We could repeat the story over again, but I think the point is made. The Eurodollar breeds on itself. It creates more and more Eurodollars. Yet, these Eurodollars are not counted when the Federal Reserve takes into its account the money supply either by M-1, M-2, or M-3. Remember, in our example, the books of the Chicago bank continued to show liabilities and assets of one million dollars (just different names), even though European banks had created $2,755,000 of new money! Of course, because of this multiplier effect, the European banks would continue to create far more money

---

*Note: It could have opened an account with any other American bank with the same net effect.

than just what we've seen before the effect of the original one million would run out. (European countries little regulate dollar denominated deposits; they do watch closely their own banking systems with regard to deposits denominated in their own currencies.)

In our example of the medieval city (Chapter 2) we learned that an increase in the money supply results in an increase in demand, which in turn drives the price of commodities up and demand for money down.

The result of the Eurodollar market is to increase the number of dollars in Europe. This, we would expect, would increase demand and force prices up. But European products are sold primarily on the basis of European currencies, not U.S. dollars. Consequently, what happens is that people with dollars convert some of them to other currencies in order to make purchases. It is this conversion of a portion of the increasing Eurodollars to foreign currencies that puts downward pressure on the U.S. dollar in exchange rates.

In actual practice, banks with dollar-denominated accounts cannot always find people to lend the money to. In that case, they send the dollars to the central bank of the country for conversion to local currency. The central bank does so and then makes a demand on the Federal Reserve of the U.S. Usually, however, the demand is not for currency, but for Treasury bills (which we saw earlier the Fed bought from the Treasury) on which foreign governments can earn interest.

Nevertheless, the Eurodollars increase in numbers over time, always exerting their subtle downward pressure on the U.S. dollar. This pressure is in the same ballpark with inflation, stagnant productivity, and deficit in trade balances. This was the situation in early 1978.

Dollar dumping

When the dollar began a sharp (but shallow) decline early in 1978 due to all the factors we've noted, something unusual happened. Large numbers of Europeans—not governments, but large businesses with cash surpluses, financial institutions, and even great numbers of private individuals—began selling Eurodollars they had on hand for stronger European currencies, primarily marks and Swiss francs. They saw the dollar was falling and they hoped to sell dollars today, buying them back in a few weeks for a profit. (This is the same situation we saw in Chapter 1 when a person traded $1,000 U.S. for 2,000 marks on Tuesday and traded back 2,000 marks for $1,020 U.S. dollars on Wednesday.)

This dumping of dollars caused additional downward pressure, which sent the price of the dollar down further and faster, causing more and more people to come into the market. Europeans used their U.S. coins, currency, and demand deposits—a huge storehouse of Eurodollars estimated at 700 billion dollars!

Of course, at any given time only perhaps a fifth or a sixth of Eurodollars are available for lending or from demand accounts (the rest are already loaned out). However, since the best estimates are that there are roughly 700 billion Eurodollars, that means that at any given time over 100 billion are available on demand deposits or for immediate lending! That's an enormous overhang, enough to turn what might have been a relatively small drop in U.S. dollar value into a plunge of catastrophic proportions.

In addition, as the dollar descended, some noticed an interesting fact. In some cases they could borrow Eurodollars from banks at fixed interest rates for short periods, exchange those dollars for Swiss francs or Deutschemarks, wait for the dollar to fall, exchange back (receiving more dollars than they paid), pay off the loan and interest with the dollars they got back, and still have a profit. As long as the dollar fell farther and faster than the interest rate charged on Eurodollar loans, there was money to be made here.

It was only President Carter's sudden and strong announcement to intervene and prop up the dollar that halted the plunge. Remember, the borrowing of Eurodollars to finance dollar sales only works as long as the dollar falls fast and far. The minute it appears the dollar will stabilize for even a short period of time, the Eurodollar supply dries up. Borrowing money to speculate with only works on sure bets. When you see the dollar fall percentage points against another currency on a daily basis, the risk seems worthwhile. But, when the dollar stabilizes for even a few days, a person gets very worried about that borrowed money he or she is gambling on and quickly pulls out of the game. (It should be noted that the process outlined here has been greatly simplified to make it understandable. In practice, interest rates on Eurodollar loans tend to reflect changes in currency rates and speculation is far riskier than it might seem here.)

A word needs to be said here about European currency habits. The countries of Europe, considered individually, are tiny compared to the United States. Most are smaller than many of our own states. And each has its own currency. Consequently, Europeans are quite used to handling a variety of different currencies and of making a little profit, when possible, on exchange rates. It's as if each state in the U.S. issued its own currencies and you exchanged every time a state border was crosssed. Very quickly Americans would come to feel right at home exchanging currencies. Enormous numbers of Europeans, including private citizens used to exchanging currency, saw the opportunity; and when the dollar plunged, they took advantage of it.

I believe that the overhang of the Eurodollar still remains and is likely to remain for some time in the future. If another sharp drop in the U.S. dollar begins (due to forces we have already discussed) the Eurodollar will be available to push it over the cliff once more.

9

Tomorrow's currency winners, today

Now that we've looked at the indicators that I think determine the values of currency, it remains to simply examine the various currencies, determine which are underpriced, buy those, collect our profits, and retire. If only life were so simple.

A lot depends on when you are reading this chapter. In the next few pages I am going to give my own personal assessment of the currency field as of this writing. You as a reader should form your own judgment (and should always check with your own personal financial advisor before making any investment).

The economic signs for the United States continue to be discouraging. There is no indication that the U.S. is significantly increasing its productivity. Remember, this is measured by the number of hours (or number of workers) required to manufacture a product. On the other hand, the wages of workers are rising. This, of course, is a consequence of inflation. If we were to measure real buying power, rather than nominal wages, we would find that today's worker is not much better off (perhaps even worse off) than the worker of a decade ago.

Inflation is currently seen as the number one enemy of the U.S. economy. This is undoubtedly the case because so much of the public is alarmed by the loss of buying power of their money. Inflation, however, is not likely to recede very much in the *immediate* future due to an important reason we'll discuss in just a moment.

Our balance of payments deficit is narrowing at the time of this writing. This is largely because the U.S. dollar's fall makes foreign currencies relatively more valuable: Our goods become less expensive for foreigners, while foreign goods become too expensive for our domestic tastes. A decade ago German and Japanese cars were among the cheapest autos that could be bought in America. Today American manufacturers are able to produce cars that compare favorably in price with imports from these same countries. The same is true for many other products. A weak dollar contributes to the narrowing of our trade deficit. On the other hand, increased costs of oil imports work to increase our deficit. Only if the U.S. were to cut its consumption of oil would it have any real hope of improving its balance of payments.

One would think that with these discouraging economic signs, the future of the dollar would be all down. That, however, is not necessarily the case. The verdict on the future of the U.S. dollar is not yet in because of two very important considerations. They are, ironically, oil and inflation. Let's consider oil first.

The U.S., as we've noted, remains one of the world's great oil producers. While oil shortages and price increases from the Middle East will surely have a harmful effect on the U.S., the effect will not be nearly as severe as in parts of Europe and in Japan where as much as 100 percent of oil used is imported. James Schlesinger as Secretary of Energy, when speaking before a congressional committee, once said that a cutoff of Mid-East oil for one year would "mean the end of the industrial world as we know it." A year's cutoff is most unlikely, but short term cutoffs, or at least reduced supplies, such as occurred during the Iranian revolt of 1978-79, are probable. During these periods of time the U.S. will be in a relatively stronger position than its European and Japanese neighbors, and the U.S. currency can be expected to reflect this strength.

Now, let's consider how inflation, strangely, could help the U.S. It has been pointed out before, but bears repeating, the U.S. has a built-in inflation killer—the progressive income tax.

It works in this fashion. As inflation gets higher, the amount of income received by individuals from jobs, professions, businesses and so forth also goes up. Great inflation means greater personal income (not necessarily greater buying power). As personal income goes up, individuals move into higher and higher tax brackets, which means that ever greater percentages of their incomes go to the government in the form of taxes. This results in the federal government's receiving increased amounts of money each year at a rate *faster* than inflation. What the government does with this money is critical.

If the government holds spending to constant levels, or even increases it just to match inflation, the government's income (increasing at a faster rate than inflation) will soon overtake its expenses. In other words, income from taxes will soon exceed expenses. This could result in a balanced budget and even a budget surplus.

If a surplus budget were used to pay off the existing national debt, that portion of the money supply being increased by the federal government could drop. Since this is a significant portion of the total money supply, it would be felt throughout the country. The effect of reducing the money supply is to reduce inflation. It's as if our mythical king in the second chapter were actually allowed to tax away the excess money in his kingdom.

Consider: The primary method of reducing inflation, according to the monetarist economic approach which this book advocates, is the reduction of the money supply. This lowers demand (consumption). This is the opposite of what we saw in Chapter 2 where increasing the money supply increased demand.

Unfortunately, in our complex economy, cutting back demand does not always reduce prices, at least not immediately. (Remember in Chapter 2 we saw that increasing demand increased price all along the demand curve. One would think that reducing demand would have the opposite effect.) It often does work in terms of basic commodities, such as orange juice. When demand is reduced, growers are not able to immediately adjust the supply. They can't grow less until at least the next season. Consequently, they must sell their present supply of oranges at the going (reduced) price in order to survive.

Reducing the demand for manufactured products, however, can actually cause the price to rise! Take automobile manufacturers as an example. When demand for cars drops, the first thing the automakers do is lay off workers at their plants. The remaining workers, however, are usually tied to relatively long-term contracts that frequently involve automatic pay increases. Reducing the work force (demand for labor) does not result in the remaining workers getting paid less. The remaining workers continue to make the same or increased wages. In addition, the manufacturer's expenses for raw materials do not drop (in the short run). Expenses for plant and equipment are fixed and must now be spread over a smaller base of car sales. Ultimately, this means that when the demand for cars drops, the unit cost of cars (in the short run) should actually rise! (In reality car manufacturers, through a complex accounting system, can absorb considerable loss in sales without having to raise individual car prices.)

What all this means is that while reducing the money supply to cut inflation does work, it does not work immediately; it takes a long time in an industrial economy. And one consequence of reduced money supply and reduced demand is unemployment. Remember, the first thing that automakers tend to do when demand for cars drops is to reduce employment. As unemployment grows, the public clamor for the federal government to "stimulate" the economy becomes thunderous.

If the government were to turn a deaf ear to this clamor, inflation could probably be whipped in a few years. However, in the past, presidents, senators, and representatives, in order to be reelected, have always listened closely to the outcry of their constituents. If more jobs are wanted, then that quickly becomes the priority over fighting inflation. How does the government stimulate the economy to provide more jobs? It increases the money supply: it spends more. The increased spending has, however, the unfortunate effect of increasing inflation.

This is not to say that high unemployment is good, while inflation is bad; rather, some unemployment may be necessary temporarily while inflation is cured.

As I said earlier, currency investors and speculators are watching to see what the U.S. does. My own observation is that no president and no Congress can long tolerate "high" unemployment. When the jobless figures pass 7 or 8 percent (remember, that means that 92 to 93 percent of the workers are still employed), all our resources are marshalled to conquer the evil of "recession."

All of which goes to show that any hopes the U.S. has of significantly reducing its inflation in the immediate future are probably pipe dreams. (Some economists believe that we now have a built-in inflation rate in our economy of between 9 and 12 percent.)

What, given these economic considerations, is the likely future of the U.S. dollar?

Over the interim period of the next four years or so or at least until 1985, I foresee continued periods of time when the dollar once again gets into trouble. This will be particularly the case if our balance-of-trade shows a big deficit.

During this period of time we can expect the following scenario to take place:

- The U.S. dollar will appear strong at times when interest rates are high in the U.S. and balance of trade is strong with foreign countries. This will be particularly true just before recessions and during the drop down.
- There will be periods when the dollar begins to falter. Interest rates in the U.S. will drop. An unfavorable balance of trade will develop. There will be a dislike for the dollar overseas. This will be generally true as the U.S. climbs out of recession into an expansionary boom period.
- Oil will affect the dollar greatly. As the OPEC countries raise prices, the inflation rate of all industrial countries will be affected. Europe could be affected more than the U.S. which would tend to strengthen the dollar.
- There may come a time when the dollar, appearing to be strong, is allowed to drift against European currencies. Sudden adverse economic news coupled with bad political news could cause the dollar to suddenly falter and then begin sliding down in value.
- If it once again topples from its "stable" position and starts downward, Europeans will be there to take advantage of the situation. The Eurodollar effect, which we noted earlier, will begin anew and the economic plug will be pulled out of the drain. The dollar will plunge until it is finally halted by exhaustion of the market, new and even more dramatic intervention, or government controls aimed at preventing anyone taking advantage of the situation.

A brief word on controls is in order here. To "stabilize" their currencies, governments can do a number of things. For example, they can restrict the amount of their currency that may be taken out of the country. Currently about 30 countries, including Australia, Great Britain, France, Italy, Japan, and South Africa, have such restrictions. Over 15 countries restrict the amount of currency you can bring in. Governments can also close exchanges and trading centers. In the long run these efforts are thwarted by the rise of black markets, but they make investing in currency difficult. Finally, governments can simply call in currency, as the U.S. did with gold in 1933.

Putting aside government controls (although keeping their possibility ever in the backs of our minds) let's return to the grim economic news we have been considering. Every coin has two sides, and grim economic news can become very happy news if you place yourself in a position to take advantage of it. Note carefully that this is not an unpatriotic position. The U.S. government has chosen not to do those things necessary to control inflation, increase production, reduce oil imports, and balance trade. It has contributed significantly to the present situation. When someone throws you overboard, you are well within your moral rights to grab for a life-preserver.

Best profit potential

Let's consider specifically where to take advantage of currency changes. (Note: in the surprising event that the indicators suddenly turn completely around and the dollar begins gaining value, there's no reason that a shrewd investor can't capitalize on the situation by selling short foreign currencies. See the next chapter.) There are more than a hundred currencies in the world. Which offers the best profit potential?

I've selected five that appeal to me. I feel these have the best chance of showing high gain during the 1980s. The reader, however, should take careful note that there is no guarantee or assurance given or implied that these currencies will, in fact, do well. No one knows the future. All five conceivably could begin dropping in value as of this writing and never recover. The reader should not rely on any recommendation given in this chapter or book, but should secure his or her own up-to-date information. Most important, the reader should not make any investment without first consulting with his or her own personal financial advisor.

Deutschemark

West Germany is and has been for some time an industrial giant in Europe. Its manufactured products include automobiles, electrical equipment, chemicals, steel products, and machinery, much of which it exports. It imports, in addition to food, the raw materials used in making its manufactured goods. Long ago the Germans came to understand that their economic survival depended on their efficiency, and they have molded themselves into a highly efficient economy.

There are about 62 million Germans living on a land area roughly equivalent in size to the state of Oregon. As we've seen, the Germans have amongst the highest productivity rates in Europe and one of the lowest inflation rates. Despite having to import great quantities of raw materials, they have consistently shown a trade surplus.

Here are the German trade figures:

Current balance—Germany
Exports/imports of merchandise, exports/imports of services, private and government unrequited transfers net.

1971	+875
1972	+747
1973	+4,371
1974	+9,804
1975	+4,059
1976	+3,902
1977	+3,799
1978	+3,000 (est.)

Source: Nov., 1978, International Financial Statistics of the International Monetary Fund.

Of course, the Germans don't have an "America-mark" problem the way the U.S. has with its "Eurodollar." For three decades, Germany has had a stable government that has shown surprising ability to administer the correct economic medicine at the appropriate time. There is no reason to suspect that Germany in the future will not be as strong or even stronger than Germany today.

The great danger is that the very strength of the German economy will price it out of world markets. A strong mark will result in higher prices for German goods elsewhere. (This is already seen by consumers in the U.S., with increased prices for German imported automobiles and cameras.) Consequently, the German government intervenes heavily in money markets to help the dollar and keep the mark from rising.

Early in 1979, largely through the urging of the German government, the effort was made to form the European Monetary System (EMS). This ostensibly was intended to link the currencies of all the Common Market nations of Europe together. The obvious reason for German interest in the plan, however, was to ensure that the mark did not price itself out of all foreign markets. Let's look at this EMS more closely.

For a number of years the Deutschemark has been linked to the currencies of four other European countries—the Netherlands, Belgium, Luxembourg, and Denmark. The "link" requires that all currencies of these countries "float" together in relation to one another. For example, if the German mark were to start to climb in relation to the Danish kroner, both the German and Danish governments would intervene to see that the mark fell and the kroner rose to previously established levels. This insures that the currencies of the different countries will maintain a relatively fixed relationship.

This doesn't mean, however, that they won't fluctuate in relation to the dollar. Rather, they move as an undulating body or "snake" in relation to the dollar. They all go up (although fluctuating within limits against each other) as the dollar falls and vice versa.

The new EMS creates a longer snake. In addition to

Germany, the Netherlands, Belgium, Luxembourg, and Denmark, it also includes France, Ireland, and Italy—all the Common Market countries with the exception of England. This would mean that the governments of each country would be required to keep their currencies probably within 2½ percent of their assigned rates at all times (except Italy which because of a higher inflation rate would undoubtedly be allowed a higher fluctuation, possibly 6 percent). By joining all these rates together it allows them all to float as a snake against the dollar.

The creation of the EMS has another aspect. By linking Germany's currency with that of other currencies, it becomes more difficult for currency speculators to influence the exchange rates. One item we have not yet dealt with is the influence of speculators. (See the next chapter on futures.) In the short run, they have been known to pick one country's currency and by timely buying and selling, force that country's currency up (or down) in relation to the dollar. The reason for this is that it's much easier to affect a single country than several. With eight currencies tied together, however, it will be extremely difficult for speculators to move them. The result is that the upward (or downward) movement of any of the currencies within the snake is likely to be less, in relation to the dollar, than currencies not tied to a snake or float. Which is to say that while the German mark may rise gradually against the dollar along with all the currencies tied to it, *big swings are unlikely.*

Of course, the fact that eight countries belong to a currency "snake" does not guarantee that one currency might not suddenly increase in value or plunge relative to its neighbors. It merely advises that all the countries involved will support (another word for intervene) any currency on which there is undue pressure. If the pressure, however, is large and long lasting, it is possible that the country involved would be obliged to pull out of the snake and either go it alone or reevaluate its currency. All of which is to say that if the other

Common Market countries' economies deteriorate while Germany's continues to become more efficient, even a snake isn't going to keep the mark down.

British pound

England is an unlikely candidate for consideration. As we've seen earlier, England has been plagued by very high inflation and low productivity. Its balance of trade has not been encouraging either, until recently.

Current balance—England
Exports/imports of merchandise, exports/imports of services, private and government unrequited transfers net.

1973	-2,298
1974	-8,254
1975	-3,932
1976	-1,833
1977	+634
1978	+500 (est.)

It is significant that recently, England's trade imbalance has switched to the plus side. It's also worth noting that the rate of inflation in England, which has been running higher than 15 percent for four years, suddenly dropped to 8 percent in 1978 before going back up.

It would appear that England may be undergoing some sort of economic transformation. In a way it is, for now England, of all countries, is modestly rich in a very important natural resource—oil. The North Sea oil has given England a decline in oil imports for the first time in memory. This, coupled with continuing manufactured exports, is what contributed to England's trade surplus.

England's biggest problem, economically, seems to be its productivity. Much of its labor force is tied to anachronistic union contracts that cripple both the quantity and the quality of production.

All of this means that England is a currency gamble. If the country can modernize and increase productivity, it could well become a leader. Consequently, the pound is a currency to watch over the first half of the decade of the 1980s, as are the English economic indicators.

SWISS FRANC

Switzerland has long been the darling of the currency investors. The Swiss franc shot up higher than any other currency during the dollar plunge of 1978. On the basis of past experience alone, it's easy to guess and bet on the Swiss franc. But, consider the indicators.

We've seen that Switzerland has in the past knocked its inflation rate down to practically zero. Its balance of payments surplus is also historically good.

Current balance—Switzerland
Exports/imports of merchandise, exports/imports of services, private and government unrequited transfers net.

1973	+280
1974	+171
1975	+2,587
1976	+3,518
1977	+3,782

As we noted in Chapter 3, the Swiss productivity has been amongst the higher in Europe. And Switzerland has one last and critically important plus on its side: For a long time it has been known as the most stable country in Europe. (It came through two devastating World Wars almost unscathed.) Today it is considered to be perhaps the world's leading financial center.

With all these pluses, how can there can be any minuses?

The answer is quite simple. As a country's currency value relative to other currencies continues to rise, it will be able to export less and less because its exports become increasingly costly to other countries. The higher the Swiss franc goes, the more difficult it is for the Swiss to export manufactured products.

This is essentially the same problem we were just discussing for Germany. However, as we've seen, Germany has taken steps to control the problem.

Switzerland, like most European countries, must export to survive. Its basic products are machinery, instruments, watches, and some steel. It also produces chemicals and pharmaceuticals. Yet, it must import almost all raw materials, fuel, and a good portion of its food. Without substantial trade, the country could not have a viable economy.

In the last few years the Swiss franc has risen in value not only in relation to the dollar, but to many other currencies. The real question is, how much longer can it continue to rise without seriously affecting trade?

I can recall back in 1976 that some economists were predicting that this problem was already catching up with the Swiss and that the SF would soon fall. Quite the opposite happened. Productivity increased and the SF shot up even further in value. This could happen again, but sometime, probably during the 1980s, the high flying Swiss franc will come to earth.

Currency buyers, therefore, should be aware that although in the short run the Swiss franc remains in contention, in the long run it could turn out to be an also-ran.

JAPANESE YEN

Japan has been a major U.S. trading partner almost since the first days after World War II. We have been Japan's biggest export consumer. (Although of late the Japanese have invaded the European market.)

As we've seen, Japan's recent inflation has been low (after

highs between 1973 and 1976). In addition, its productivity is high and increasing. Japan showed a very high deficit in trade during 1974 (-$5,942 billion U.S.) but since then has bounced back and saw an incredible +$10,911 billion in 1977.

Japan's great problem has always been oil. Although it has held its increase in consumption of oil down to only 10 percent between 1975 and 1977, the price of oil still takes its toll. This may be offset by the mid-1980s, however, by new trade agreements between Japan and the People's Republic of China, not to re-mention the new inroads Japanese products have made in the European markets.

In my opinion, the Japanese yen continues to be underpriced relative to the dollar and many European currencies. It continues to be a good currency bet in both the long and the short run. But, the yen is volatile—it is not an Asian SF.)

MEXICAN PESO

Mexico is a land of mystery, both culturally and economically. Mexico does not release much economic information as compared to other countries which readily supply figures. For example, it is difficult to know any facts about the Mexican labor force. Some estimates, however, have indicated unemployment runs as high as 20 to 40 percent!) Monetary information is also difficult to come by, even though the following information is presumed to be reliable.

Current balance—Mexico
Exports/imports of merchandise, exports/imports of services, private and government unrequited transfers net.

1973	-1,415
1974	-2,876
1975	-4,042
1976	-3,420
1977	-2,068

Source: Nov., 1978, International Financial Statistics, International Monetary Fund.

In comparison to the countries we've looked at thus far, these figures are not encouraging. It's impossible to judge Mexican productivity; however, it probably is dismally low. Inflation also, as we saw earlier, is very high, although not as high as for many other Central and South American countries.

As if this were not enough, Mexico is faced with a long-term problem that may be unresolvable—its birth rate. It has been estimated reliably that by the turn of the century, Mexico's population will be close to 100 million.

In the past Mexico's great industry, besides tourism, has been its agricultural products. One way of handling increased population might be to grow more food. However, since the Mexican revolution, a promise has been given to the Mexican people that they will own their own land. This has resulted in successive administrations turning over good agricultural land to small family farms. In some cases, this land was taken from large successful growers. While this may be good sense from a political, social, and even moral position, it is economic disaster. Small farm units, as the U.S. long ago learned, are highly inefficient. In order to produce food in great quantity and quality, large farms are needed.

The return to small farms only means increased poverty for the population as a whole. The combination of skyrocketing population coupled with the dream of every citizen of owning land has led in large part to Mexico's current state of discomfort. Here's the history of the Mexican peso relative to the U.S. dollar:

Pesos to one U.S. dollar

1971	12.5
1972	12.5
1973	12.5
1974	12.5
1975	12.498
1976	18.95 (devaluation)
1977	22.736

Although in the past the dollar did badly against the Japanese and some European currencies, it did smashingly well against the Mexican peso. This was not, however, good news to some Americans. Mexican banks have long paid much higher interest rates than American banks. Consequently, some Americans placed their money in Mexican financial institutions in pesos. When the currency was devalued, these Americans lost a great deal of their capital. There is nothing I or anyone else can say that could convince them to consider Mexico again as an investment area.

Mexico should be considered, however, for one very important reason—oil. As of this writing, Mexico counts its *proven* oil reserves at 40 billion barrels. That makes it the world's sixth largest oil-rich country. Since discovery of Mexican oil fields has been fairly recent, it may turn out that eventually Mexican oil reserves could be even larger.

Oil, as we've seen, is money—better than money. Mexico is just now developing its oil fields, and it will be several years before substantial production takes place. But, once it does, the economic indicators for Mexico may shift abruptly.

A word needs to be said here about oil production. Oil production is not labor-intensive. That is, it does not require a great quantity of labor to bring the oil out of the ground. Consequently, it has been argued that oil production will not directly help the average Mexican citizen. Most oil workers, in fact, may be foreign, highly trained laborers.

That is not entirely true. Mexican oil is nationalized under Pemex; much of the profits will go to the national treasury. It depends on how the government spends the money as to how the citizens benefit.

One hears a lot of horror stories about Mexican bureaucracy. (Having spent considerable time in the country, I suggest that many of them are true.) However, in recent decades the top Mexican federal government has been consistently pledged and determined to promote the welfare of the country and its population. In government after government, however, the problems were overwhelming and the resources pitifully small. In the near future, for perhaps the first time, the resources may be sufficient. It, of course, remains to be seen if the Mexican government will use the new resources with the same dedication former governments exhibited.

All of which is to say that Mexico has the potential to cut its inflation and reverse its trade balance. (Productivity remains hopeless in the foreseeable future.) This can mean a reversal in the direction of the Mexican peso. If it even climbs back to where it was in 1974, it will mean an increase in value of about 40 percent, relative to the U.S. dollar! That's an enormous swing and makes the peso an absolute must for currency watchers. (But, be careful, it could go down even further before it goes up.)

We've covered five countries and their currencies with whirlwind speed. The reader should understand that no effort has been made at completeness. It should be obvious that this entire book could easily be devoted to each country and still not cover the subject. I've covered the highlights or the particularly significant indicators and facts for me. Once again, I emphasize, as I did at the beginning of this chapter, the reader should seek out his or her own information and then, never act without first seeking the advice of a personal financial advisor.

One last point should be mentioned on government intervention. We've noted elsewhere that governments intervene in currency markets by buying and selling; that they can establish fixed rates of exchange and declare any other rates illegal; that they can restrict the amount of currency you may be allowed to bring into or out of a country; and that they can announce any other restrictive measures they deem necessary.

Usually this results in the opening of black markets. If you're seriously thinking about dealing in black markets, think again. Not only is it illegal, it can mean economic and personal disaster for the unlucky participant.

What's important to note here is that if you get committed

to a currency and, while so committed, a government (perhaps including our own) clamps down a restrictive ruling, you might lose all or a portion of your investment. Don't say it won't happen. In 1933 the U.S. government prohibited U.S. citizens from owning gold. All U.S. citizens were required to turn in any gold bullion or coins they owned (except those with numismatic value). If things get rough, the government could unexpectedly do the same thing again.

Does that mean you shouldn't invest? Hardly. It just means that you should be aware of the risks of investment.

10
The currency futures game

THE EASIEST and perhaps the safest method of investing in currency is to go to your local currency exchanger and trade U.S. dollars for yen or Swiss francs or whatever. Then, you simply wait for the price of the foreign currency to rise, relative to the dollar, and when it does you exchange back and collect your profit. As we saw in Chapter 1, this is the simple method that travelers to foreign countries use. It is also a method that many Europeans use to invest in currency. Of course, you don't always win. If it turns out that the dollar rises and the currency you bought falls, you lose. You do, however, have alternatives. You can hang on to your purchase indefinitely waiting for the market to change, or you can sell and take your loss immediately.

Commodity exchanges

There is another method that offers unlimited profits . . . and unlimited risks. Trading in currency futures. As we saw in Chapter 2, money is a commodity and so, naturally enough, money or currency is traded on commodity markets right along with pork bellies, coffee, and wheat. Not all the currencies of the world are traded, however. Usually it's just those that are most active such as the Deutschemark, Swiss franc, British pound, Japanese yen, Canadian dollar, and, perhaps, the Mexican peso. (On some markets the French franc and Dutch guilder are also actively traded.) There are commodity markets across the country and around the world. Some of the largest are in Chicago and include the International Monetary Market of the Chicago Mercantile Exchange. New York has its New York Mercantile Exchange. There is a Mid-American Commodity Exchange and so on. Where you trade is not that critical as long as the place has an active market—that is, there is a lot of trading going on.

Finding a broker

What is critical is that you find and develop a trusting and working relationship with a good commodities broker. Trading in futures is a complex endeavor and in this chapter we're just going to skim the surface. We'll point out some of the things that can be done and a few of the pitfalls. But, before you invest a penny you should read all you can on the subject (see the last chapter for sources of material) and, I repeat, find a good commodities broker.

How do you know a good commodities broker? It's not always easy. He or she should have been in the business long enough to have made all the mistakes. That way the broker can save you from making them. I would think five years active commodity trading would be a minimum requirement. The broker should work for a firm large enough to have seats on various commodity exchanges so your order can be placed without delay. It should be large enough to afford the latest computers which will show at a moment's glance the current and future prices of commodities you are interested in.

Besides experience and working for a substantial firm, your broker should be intelligent, aware of the market from moment to moment, and pleasant to talk with. These latter qualities you'll also have to judge for yourself; a good way to do it is to go down to the broker's office on several occasions before buying anything and have chats with him or her. A good broker won't mind your taking up some time, provided you don't come early or late in the trading day when the market is likely to be most active.

Listen carefully to what your broker says. Remember, a broker isn't paid a salary like a carpenter or a banker. He or she survives by making a commission on each transaction. Be a bit wary of brokers who try to get you into the market by suggesting that you quickly make a series of rapid-fire transactions. This may make you money. Or, it might simply fatten the broker's commissions.

One of the most important functions a broker can handle for you is the management of your investment money. Knowing or having a belief that a particular currency is going to make a large movement is really only half the battle. Understanding the daily trading range, limiting exposure, getting out with your profit—that is, using the market to take advantage of your belief—is the other half. A good money manager can go a long way toward helping you here. The crucial thing is to have a plan or approach toward investing in finances.

One money manager I know, Bob Kreuter of Costa Mesa, California, always asks his clients to answer three questions for him before investing:

1. Why am I buying or selling? (Do I have a belief that a particular currency is going to go up or down?)

2. At what point do I get out of the market if my belief turns out to be wrong? (See the section on stop-loss orders in this chapter.)

3. At what point do I get out of the market if my belief turns out to be correct?

These are three excellent questions you should always ask yourself before you invest in the futures market. It is easy enough to say that you'll enter with a trend (when the price starts going up, or down) and get out when the trend turns the other way. But, identifying that trend from moment to moment in midstream is difficult. (One definition of a trend which I found useful to remember is that a trend is something which started yesterday and will end tomorrow.)

As I mentioned, it is important to have a plan. You should have a specific price at which you'll get out, no matter what. If you're wrong and the market goes against you, you'll take your loss and get out, hoping for success next time. Similarly, if you're winning, you'll bail out at an appropriate time. For example, you might go into the market wanting to double your money (an understandable goal). Your initial investment may be $5,000 and you agree with yourself that you'll get out if and when you reach $10,000. If you should be fortunate enough to reach your mark, I guarantee a little voice will pop into your ear and say, "Stick with it, you'll make $20,000!"

Many commodity advisors will agree with that little voice and urge you to stick with your winner, play it for all it's worth. For myself, I say that better judgment is to get out when I've reached my goal. If I've made the 100 percent profit I set out to make, I'll leave. This, of course, doesn't mean I can't immediately reinvest in the same currency and try to double my money again. It only means that I'm determined to walk away from the game a winner. It is positively appalling how many investors make huge profits at the commodities "game" and then don't leave, instead plowing their winnings right back in until they're all gone. It's as important to be a profit-taker as a loss-avoider.

It's also important to remember that it is in the nature of commodities trading to deal with volatility. Prices move up and down, not just on a daily basis, but on a moment to moment basis. And there are always tipsters around to fill your ears with the right answer to what's going to happen next. Be wary of such individuals, particularly if they wear broker's clothes. As we've noted earlier, no one knows what's going to happen in the future.

Unless you just want to have fun playing the futures market (and many people do) and can afford to hire a competent brokerage firm to manage an account for you, I suggest you spend a good deal of time personally investigating your prospective broker. Find someone you like and can trust and then work with him or her. You'll improve your chances considerably.

One last word of caution before we consider futures trading. This is a risky business. You can lose your money by bad investment or you can see some of your profit and capital eaten away in broker's fees. This doesn't mean that you can't make big profits. You can. But, you can also suffer unlimited losses. All of which goes to say that you shouldn't even think of entering the commodities market as a speculator (a term to be explained shortly) unless you enter it with high-risk money—money that you can afford to lose without affecting your style of life or your regular source of income. And never, never enter the market with borrowed money. (Generally speaking, high-risk money is usually considered to be no more than 5 to 10 percent of your net worth.)

How much is a minimum investment? I've heard knowledgeable people say that one shouldn't enter the market with less than $50,000. Others emphasize that $5,000 is the minimum necessary. Usually the reason for giving minimums such as these is the fact that before you win, you may lose many times. And you will need sufficient capital to see you through the losses. As for myself, I don't feel that there is any minimum or maximum amount (other than the minimums set by brokerage firms), as long as you can handle a loss, walk away and not feel it's the end of the world. (Your loss, however, may not be limited only to the amount you initially invest. Your loss potential, just as your profit potential, is basically unlimited. If you make a bad move and you can't get out of the market, it could be very expensive indeed!) It's sort of the same psychology used in gambling. Never gamble with more than you can afford to lose.

Now, let's see just what the futures market is all about.

Forward pricing

Let's consider the case of an American importer of Japanese transistorized modulefams. (You've never heard of a modulefram? It doesn't matter.) Our importer goes to Japan where he consults with the modulefram manufacturer. He is confident he can sell them in the American market, provided, of course, the price is right. As it turns out the price the Japanese manufacturer wants is a good one. He wants 1,200 yen per modulefram provided our importer buys a minimum of 10,000 of them (12,000,000 yen). The exchange rate on the day the deal is made is 200 yen to 1 dollar. Our importer, therefore, knows he's buying the modulefams for 6 dollars apiece or the whole lot for $60,000. Since he can sell them for $8 apiece in the U.S., it's a good deal.

Now, a problem arises. The manufacturer has agreed to deliver the modulefams to the United States by the cheapest way possible. That turns out to be by freighter. But, she estimates that it will take six months for the ship to arrive. Our importer stresses that he won't pay until he gets delivery. This, of course, means that he will have to pay the 12,000,000 yen to the manufacturer in six months. But, what if the exchange rate changes in six months? What if, for example, during that time period it drops to 150 yen to the dollar? That would mean that our importer would have to pay $80,000 U.S. (12,000,000 yen divided by 150) an increase of $20,000 U.S. This might very well wipe out any profit he had hoped to make.

How can our importer sign a contract today, accept delivery, and make payment six months hence with any assurance that he won't lose all his profit through changes in the currency exchange rate? One answer is the futures market. (Banks also provide forward pricing services.)

In the futures market our importer can "lock" the price of yen six months in the future without actually exchanging dollars for yen today. Here's how he goes about doing it. His first step is to contact a commodities broker and to explain what he wants. It turns out that the broker he contacts is affiliated with the Enormous Mercantile Exchange which does handle futures in yen. The minimum contract, however, is 12,500,000 yen or $62,500 at a 200 yen to 1 U.S. dollar ratio. Our importer says the extra 500,000 yen doesn't matter and to go ahead and purchase a contract.

The next step is the deposit. The broker explains that our importer must come up with a deposit as a sign of good faith. We'll discuss the deposit more in a moment, but for now let's just assume that it is $5,000. Our importer deposits with the broker the $5,000. The broker calls in a buy order to his representative who is "seated" on the floor of the exchange and, by calling out his offer to purchase, finds a seller agreeable to selling 12,500,000 yen for delivery six months in the future at a price agreed upon today. A contract is "opened." The price, it turns out, is 198 yen to the dollar. When the importer points out that the current (called the "spot") exchange rate is 200 to 1, the broker explains that future prices always are slightly different from spot prices depending on anticipation of what the market will do and upon the differences in interest rates between countries.

Now our importer waits. Close to the end of six months he exchanges dollars for yen. It turns out that yen are being exchanged in the ratio of 190 to 1 dollar. To deliver 12,000,000 yen to pay for moduleframs it costs him $63,157.89. In this transaction he has lost $3,157.89 by waiting the six months before making payment.

At the same time he calls his commodity broker and tells him to sell his contract. Since the delivery date of the contract is virtually at hand, the price is almost the same as the spot exchange rate (we'll discuss why, shortly) so the broker sells the contract for 12,500,000 yen at a ratio of 190 to 1 or $65,789.47. You'll recall the purchase price *of the contract* was $62,500. When we subtract the purchase from the selling price of the contract we find that the importer made $3,289.47 on his futures contract. The broker delivers this amount to him along with the original $5,000 deposit, subtracting only $100 for brokerage fees.

When our importer subtracts the $3,157.89 he lost by waiting six months on the spot market from this $3,189.47 (includes the $100 deducted for brokerage fees), he finds that he actually made a small profit of $32.39.

Of course, the small profit is not what matters here. (It might just as well have been a small loss.) What matters to the importer is the fact that by having two separate transactions—one involving the actual exchange of currency, the other involving the buying and later selling of a future contract—he was able to avoid a loss on the purchase of moduleframs due to changing currency rates. Technically speaking our importer was "hedging" or setting a future price to protect himself. Hedging is a common word we all use. We often hear it expressed as "hedging a bet." The meaning is the same in our usage.

When our importer bought a contract, it was "opened." It was "offset" or "closed out" when he sold it. Note carefully that in this example our importer *did not take delivery of the 12,500,000 yen purchased in the future contract*. Rather than accept delivery, he exchanged dollars for yen at the spot exchange rate and separately closed out his contract. These were two totally distinct transactions. The importer exchanged dollars for yen to pay for moduleframs. He bought and sold a futures contract in order to hedge his purchase against changing exchange rates. Hedging, therefore, is only a temporary substitute for the actual cash transaction. In theory, of course, our importer could have taken delivery of the yen by demanding it on his futures contract. (And sometimes this is advisable.) This, however, would have meant that the person who sold him the yen would have to, on the delivery date, go to an exchanger and exchange dollars (francs, Deutschemarks, or whatever) for yen and deliver them to our importer. To avoid this inconvenience our importer simply closed out the contract. In actual practice *only between 2 and 3 percent of futures contracts ever accept delivery.*

Our example raises an interesting point. Who was this person who sold the yen to the importer and then, if delivery was demanded, had to go out and buy them in order to fulfill the contract? Did this person actually have the gall to sell 12,500,000 yen without actually owning them?

Yes, he did. In the futures market it is not necessary to own a commodity, such as currency, in order to sell it.

This is perhaps the most difficult concept to grasp when it comes to dealing with futures. Let's try to come to terms with it by going back to our importer. When our importer executed a "buy" order for yen he was establishing what is technically known as a "long" position. He contracted to buy, promising to pay on delivery, putting up a deposit or earnest money amount. No one asked him at the time if he indeed had the $62,500 U.S., which is what he contracted to come up with in six months. No one cared. Remember that deposit we were speaking of. Let's look at it a bit more closely now.

Security deposit

The security deposit was actually required in order to cover any initial loss our importer may have had on his contract due to adverse changes in the exchange rate. In our example, we assumed that over the course of the six-month period the ratio of yen to dollars never got higher than 200 to 1. As long as it remained at this ratio or lower, our importer could always have sold the contract for what he paid for it, minus any commission.

If, however, the ratio rose to more than 200 to 1, then it

would cost him more to sell the contract than he paid for it. For example, at 201 yen to $1 U.S., 12,500,000 yen exchanged back to dollars only yields $62,189.05. Since our importer paid $62,500, this change of only ½ percent in the ratio means a loss of $311.50. Where would this money come from? It would come out of the security deposit.

The amount of the deposit required is determined in part by the commodity exchange and in part by the brokerage house and it reflects the risk involved. The risk is determined by the maximum amount a commodity can fall in value in a single trading day. (Note: When the yen goes from 200 to 201 to 1 dollar, it is a loss in value *for the yen*. Since our importer has locked in the price of yen relative to the dollar, it is also a loss for him.) These limits are geared to the previous day's price of yen. Let's say that the maximum limit for the yen is $750. If it were to drop $750 U.S. in value, trading would halt. The $750 would be deducted from our importer's security account. Trading would begin on the next trading day and if the yen suddenly shot back up the limit, $750 would be added back to our importer's account.

It should be apparent that over a number of days the account can be substantially increased or decreased depending on the price of the yen. If it is increased over the initial deposit, this money is considered profit and may be withdrawn by the importer on a daily basis. (In our example, the importer left it in for the full term of the contract and drew it out in a single sum—his profit of $3,289.47—less commission.) If it is decreased over the course of the contract, more and more is taken out of the security deposit. In our case, the original margin was $5,000 and the maintenance margin was $2,000. When the yen drops in value it begins wiping out the maintenance margin. When it falls far enough to totally deplete the maintenance margin, in our case a loss of $2,000, the broker calls the importer and informs him that he must replenish the full maintenance margin—bring his total deposit back up to $5,000. This means coming up immediately with $2,000. If the importer fails to do this, the broker immediately sells the contract and prevents both the importer and the brokerage house from sustaining any further loss. (We'll see shortly how to avoid margin calls.) The importer has his contract closed out, loses $2,000, has the remaining $3,000 returned to him (assuming that the broker was able to timely sell the contract). In this fashion it is unnecessary for the importer to ever have the $62,500 original total value of the contract. When it drops below his maintenance margin, it is sold. All he needs to have is enough money for the initial security deposit.

An interesting sidelight to this occurs when there are big swings in the currency market. For example, the yen might fall dramatically on bad news. After $750 the limit would be reached and trading stopped. However, the next day when the market opened, there might not be any buyers at prices close to the previous day's trading. The price would immediately fall another $750. And so on for several days or even a week or so, until buyers close to the previous day's trading are found. A buyer in such a market might not be able to get out as the price fell the limit each day. This could eat up the original deposit (margin) and additional money to boot. It might mean that the importer could not only lose his security deposit, but be committed to the brokerage house for additional funds.

The speculator

At this point, the reader should have at least some grasp of how it is possible to buy a futures contract without really having the cash to make the purchase. If not, then I suggest a rereading of the last few pages. If so, then you are ready to understand how it is possible to sell something you don't have. It is done in the same way as buying.

The person who sold the contract our importer purchased (who agreed to sell 12,500,000 yen for $62,500 U.S.) might have been a speculator. This is not the derisive term some readers may feel it is. Read on. We'll say our speculator is Myra. Myra felt that the yen was going to lose value, relative to the dollar, in the future. This is the same thing as saying the dollar was going to gain strength relative to the yen. To take advantage of her belief, she might have bought dollars if she were in a European country or in Japan. But, since she was in the U.S., the easiest way for her to take advantage of a possible rise in the value of the dollar relative to the yen was to sell yen. She ordered her broker to sell yen six months in the future. Just as our importer didn't have to come up with $62,500 immediately in order to buy, Myra didn't have to come up with 12,500,000 yen in order to sell. She only had to come up with a deposit of $5,000. If she was right and the yen fell in value, her profit would be deposited to her account and she could withdraw it daily. If she was wrong (as was the case in our example), her loss would be taken out of her maintenance deposit. When that was depleted, she would have to replenish it or the broker would close out her contract to protect both Myra and the broker and house from further loss. Just as our importer only needed the security deposit to buy yen, Myra needs only a security deposit to sell yen. Buying is termed opening a "long" position. Selling is termed opening a "short" position.

From this brief discussion it should be apparent that for every buyer there must be a seller.

An observant reader might ponder the following apparent inconsistency. Our importer, who in our example was making money, would want to hold his long position for the next six months. But, Myra, since she guessed wrong, would want to close out her position very quickly, perhaps in just a few weeks. How can our importer maintain his contract for six months when Myra closes out her end of it in just a few weeks?

The answer is that when Myra closes out the contract her broker does so by finding another speculator (or it could be a Japanese importer, who is hedging and wants to buy dollars and sell yen). Each commodity exchange maintains a clearinghouse that reconciles all trades on each day of trading. The clearinghouse assumes opposite sides of the trade for both the original buyer and seller, and in this fashion always balances out each contract.

If you think it's a complicated process, it is . . . and please be aware that we are barely scratching the surface. What's important to understand here is the principle of selling "short." That is selling a commodity without really owning it. Once you've found a competent broker, he or she can help you over the mechanical hurdles involved in the actual trades.

Let's get back to Myra, the speculator. What function has she fulfilled in the trade? Our importer did not want to bear the risk of fluctuating currency rates during the six months between the time he signed the contract for moduleframs and accepted delivery and made payment. So he entered the commodities market in currency. Yet, entering the market did not eliminate the risk. The risk of price fluctuations was always present. What our importer actually did was transfer the risk from himself to someone else. In this case, the risk was transferred to Myra. She was willing to accept the risk of a changing currency rate, a risk which might result in her losing money, for the chance that she might make money on the deal. Myra wouldn't make a profit for nothing. She was the risk-taker. The risk-taker in a commodities market is called the speculator.

From this point of view, a speculator has an important, even critical, function in commodities trading. Without the speculator, the market could not function efficiently. It takes lots of speculators to balance off the contracts desired by hedgers. If only hedgers, such as our importer, were in the market, it would be a static market—one in which buying or selling a contract would be difficult. It is the presence of speculators that makes the market fluid. That, in a very real sense, makes it work.

That's why there's nothing wrong with being called a

commodity speculator. It is a title of distinction and of value. And the next time someone uses it derisively, you can explain why it shouldn't be used in such fashion.

The hedger

Before we go on to examine the market itself, let's consider one other kind of hedger—a money hedger. One type of investor we haven't much discussed is the interest rate chaser—individuals as well as financial institutions that move money from country to country in search of the highest interest rates. These people also use the futures market to hedge their investment. They want to be sure that the profit they make on interest is not lost when they exchange currencies.

Let's consider an example. We'll suppose that 90-day certificates of deposit in England are bringing 12 percent annual interest, while in the United States they are bringing only 9 percent interest. It only makes good business sense to invest money in the English certificates and receive an additional 3 percent interest. Let's say a banker has $950,000 U.S., which he exchanges for 475,000 British pounds sterling (exchange rate is £1 = $2 U.S.) and which he then uses to buy 12 percent, 90-day C.D.s. At the end of 90 days he collects his 475,000 British pounds plus 12 percent annual interest, which for 90 days equals £14,250. If the exchange rate has remained at £1 = $2 U.S., when he converts back to dollars he will have $28,500 or an extra $7,018 made by investing in England.

Investing $950,000 in the U.S. at 9 percent for 90 days = $21,482
Investing £475,000 in Britain at 12 percent for 90 days = $28,500
   Extra interest made by investing in England = $7,018

Let's suppose, however, that during this same 90-day period the exchange ratio of the pound to the dollar dropped to 1.98 to 1. What happens when our investor converts back to dollars? He started with £475,000 pounds and made interest of £14,250 for a total of £489,250 to be converted back. When the conversion is made (£489,250 x 1.98) he gets back $969,000 U.S. Since he started with $950,000 U.S., his profit is $19,000 U.S. This could prove to be most embarrassing to our investor, however. As we just noted, by simply investing the same money in the U.S. for 90 days at 9 percent interest, he could have made $21,482. By going to England he lost $2,482 in potential interest. The exchange rate did him in.

Any smart investor, however, would not jump countries unless he could hedge his investment in the futures market. Our investor was not stupid and he did make such a hedge. On the day he exchanged dollars for pounds and bought the 90-day C.D., he also sold 2 million pounds forward three months. The ratio of the exchange for the future contract was £1.99 to $1 U.S.

(Note: In theory the difference in interest rates between countries should be reflected exactly in the differences between the spot price and the future price of currency, "interest rate parity." For example, if England's interest rate was 3 percent higher than in the U.S., the future price of British pounds should be discounted exactly 3 percent on a 12-month contract. In actual practice, however, restraints on trade or currency and anticipated changes in currency rates also affect future rates. It is more appropriate to say that future rates *tend* toward "interest rate parity.")

Our investor sold 500,000 pounds at 1.99 to 1, or $995,000 U.S. equivalent. Three months later he closed out his contract by buying 500,000 pounds, for roughly 198 to 1. (As the futures delivery date gets closer to the present, the difference between the futures rate and the spot rate tends to zero, which makes sense since the future is rapidly becoming the present.) He sold for $995,000 U.S. equivalent and bought for U.S. $990,000 equivalent. That's $5,000 profit. When this $5,000 profit in the futures market is compared to the $2,482 loss in the spot market transaction, our investor comes out $2,518 to the good. Of course, in actual practice he might have made more money. Or less.

Long/short

Two things should be observed from these examples. First is the fact that money investors tend to chase higher interest rates. (Those who benefit from taking advantage of interest rate disequilibrium are called arbitrageurs.)

Secondly, it is possible to make money whether the market is going up or whether it is going down.

Perhaps Chart 10A will remove any lingering confusion the reader may have about selling short.

CHART 10A Long and short of the futures market

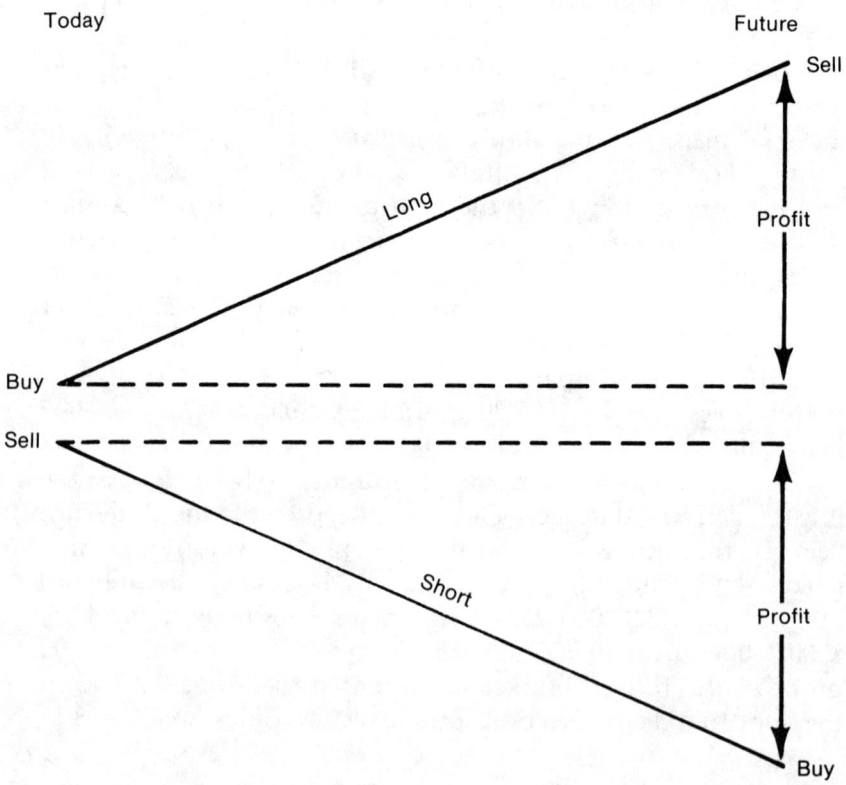

Remember, the key to understanding long and short is to understand that you don't need to own the commodity or the cash to fulfill the contract at the time you open it. You only need enough for the security deposit.

All of which goes to say that movement in the futures market does not occur in a straight line, but rather in an infinite number of ups and downs. This is caused by all the fundamental influences on currency which we saw earlier in this book, and by the effects of thousands upon thousands of hedgers, arbitrageurs, and speculators. As we mentioned earlier, a graph of the commodities market for currency looks much more like a sawtooth (left below) than a butter knife (right below).

Calculating market movements

Given the fact that the market overall may trend in a certain direction, it should be clear that in the short run and in the very short run, it may go in the opposite direction. This can spell disaster for a beginning investor. Consider the following price history of a newly created currency we'll call golads (see Chart 10B).

It should be immediately apparent that although golads have over the long run trended higher and higher, in the short run they have fallen many times. This means that an investor could make money both by taking long and short positions depending on when. A long position from A to B on our graph would yield a profit. A short position from C to D also would yield a profit. If the positions were opposite, however,

152 Buying and selling currency for profit

CHART 10B Golad price history

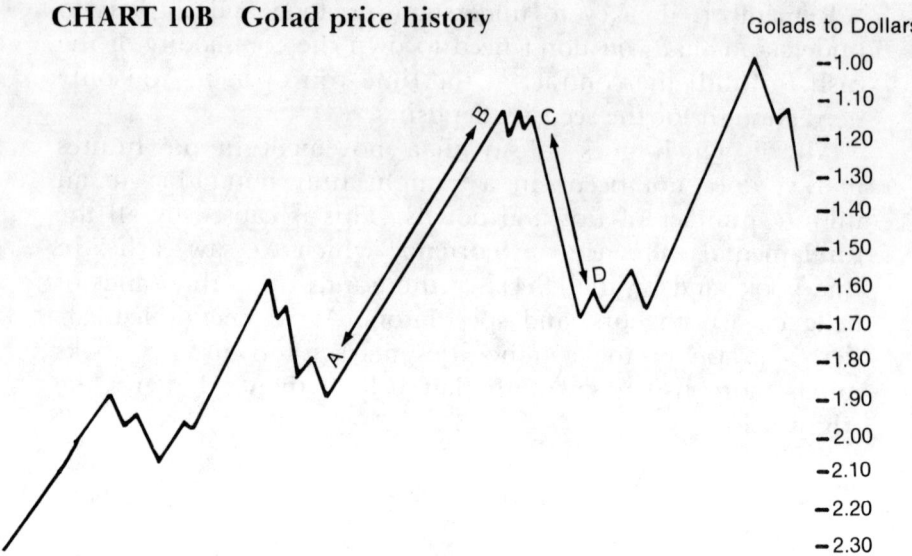

losses would result. Timing is everything. Let's consider golads more closely.

Let's suppose we believe that golads are going to increase in value over the dollar in the long run. In order to take advantage of our hunch, we will buy golads now when it is, for example, 2 to the dollar, and sell later when, we hope, it is 1 to the dollar. We'll further assume that the minimum contract is 50,000 golads or $25,000 U.S. Our security deposit is $5,000. When the golads jump in value to 1 to the dollar, we'll make $25,000 profit or 500 percent!

The week after we buy the golads, they fall in value to 2.5 to 1 dollar. This wipes out our deposit and we show a loss. The next week, however, the golads make a surprising comeback and shoot up all the way to 1 golad to $1 U.S. We, however, because we already lost all our investment capital, can't take advantage of the situation. We were right in our assessment of what was going to happen to the goladium market. However, our timing was one week off. A temporary downward fluctuation wiped out our chances of taking advantage of the upward trend we guessed correctly was coming. Could we have avoided this problem?

Stop-loss

Perhaps. Probably the most useful tool of the investor in the futures market is the "stop-loss" order. It is quite simple. We instruct our broker that after we have opened a position, if we begin losing money, he is to close out our position upon a certain maximum loss. For example, we might have said that after $500 of our deposit was lost, the broker should immediately sell the golads. Incurring a $500 loss indicates, to us, that we were on a downward fluctuation while betting on an upward trend. We were fighting the market; and while the market may not always be "right," it always is more powerful.

The result of our $500 stop-loss order is that instead of losing our $5,000, we only lose $500. When golads stop their downward fluctuation and start upward again, we can once more buy into the market. All of which goes to say that by executing stop-loss orders, we can have many chances ($5,000 ÷ $500 = 10 chances) at hitting the upward trend instead of just one.

Does this mean we're bound to succeed? No. Only that we've improved the odds. We could guess wrong ten times. If we did, however, there are two conclusions that any reasonable person could probably draw. The first is that our guess of an upward trend is probably wrong. And second, we're making our broker a bit richer for he gets a commission on each contract. (Note, brokers get only one commission per contract—one commission for both opening and closing a position. The commission is, so to speak, for a roundtrip ticket.)

Market orders

There are a number of other orders to our broker that should be understood. The order that we've been assuming on all our transactions so far is an "at the market" order. It simply means to buy or sell immediately at the best price possible. A different kind of order is a "limit order." This can limit the price to be paid either for buying or selling, or it can limit the *time* period. For example, a limit order might be to buy a yen contract at 200 to 1 within the next four hours. The broker has four hours to get the desired price or better; after that the contract order is cancelled.

An "open order" specifies the price to be paid, but does not restrict the time. It is frequently seen when a speculator believes that an upward or downward trend is coming. The speculator instructs the broker to buy when the currency reaches a certain level. For example, if trading is currently at 200 to 1, a speculator may feel an upward trend is starting when it increases in value to 198 to 1. (The assumption is that if it goes to 198 to 1, it'll go a lot further, perhaps to 190 to 1 or more.) Consequently, the broker is instructed to "open" a contract only if the price reaches 198 to 1.

A "day order" requires that it must be executed on the day designated or it is automatically cancelled. Normally all orders are considered day orders unless specific instructions are given otherwise.

At this point, the need for a good broker should be apparent. The broker must be willing to execute exactly the order you specify and must be sufficiently on top of the market at all times in order to be able to execute it efficiently and properly.

Technical analysis

One big question remains and that is, how can one know when a currency is going to fluctuate up or down? Of course, one can't know for sure, but an entire field of study is devoted to making good guesses.

Thus far, we've been using a fundamental approach to currency. We've analyzed what causes exchange rates to change and how to make educated guesses on future trends. Even in the short run we've noted that economic news can affect currency rates. But, there is another way of looking at currency. Instead of considering "why," this method considers "patterns."

Chart 10C depicts a technical analysis of golads over a four-year period.

CHART 10 C   Golad technical analysis

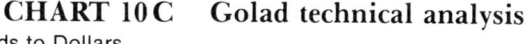

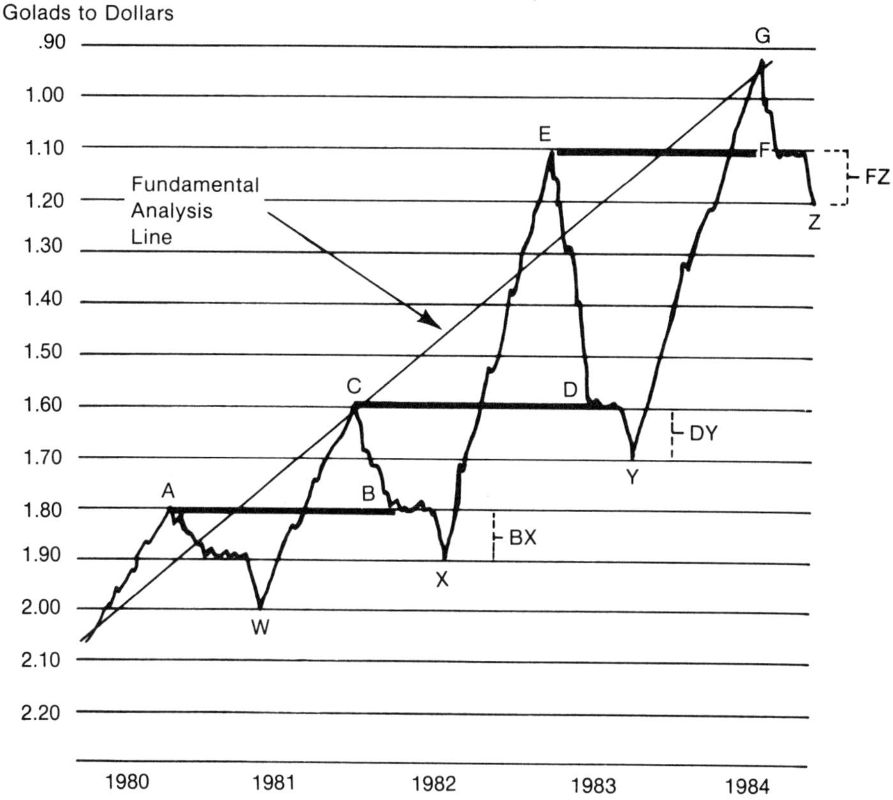

A fundamental analysis is indicated by the straight arrow. It might show that over the long run golads are going to trend upward. A technical analysis, however, might focus on those areas indicated by straight horizontal bars and circles.

156 Buying and selling currency for profit

Note the areas A through G. Each horizontal bar, A to B, C to D, and E to F, tells us something very significant. Golads had four major upward and downward fluctuations. In the last four years, each downward plunge fell until it reached a plateau which happened to coincide with the highest previous peak. After reaching the peak C, goladium fell to the plateau B, which just happened to coincide with its previous major high, A. After the peak E, the fall to plateau D just happened to coincide with the previous peak C. After the peak G, the fall to plateau F just happened to coincide with the previous peak E. After each peak, there was a fall to a plateau which coincided with the previous peak.

Even more interesting is that after the plateau, the value of golads always plunged an additional .10 before the bottom was reached and it started up again, BX, DY, FZ.

What does this analysis tell us about golads? Its most recent peak was G. It then fell to plateau F which coincides with the previous peak E just as it had done before. And at the present time it is exactly 10 cents lower, the point at which the bottom of the plunge had been reached on three previous occasions. On the basis of this technical analysis alone, even though golads are on the downward trend, now is the time to buy because very soon, perhaps tomorrow, it will start upward.

The value of technical analysis should be apparent from this hypothetical example. Unfortunately, very few markets behave in such orderly fashion. Usually the pattern is very difficult to discern, if, in fact, one does exist. Another thing to keep in mind is that just because it's happened before, doesn't mean it will happen again. It might turn out that the golad currency has just been devalued due to inflation and loss of productivity in the country of Goladium. Instead of stopping at 190 (on our chart) it might plunge all the way to 120 or lower. Of course, we would have instituted a stop order to prevent our losing all our money.

The technical analysis of specific currencies is an enormous subject and an important one. As we've noted earlier, occasionally trends will be so obvious that a fundamental analysis alone will be enough to allow success in the market. In most cases, however, a combination of fundamental and technical analysis is necessary. Technical analysis, however, is a very broad subject and one that normally requires constant updating. It is beyond the scope of this introductory discussion to deal with it thoroughly. It is suggested, therefore, that speculators consult with their commodities broker for sources of the latest up-to-date technical information before making a futures investment.

Peaks and valleys

In our example of goladium we were trying to find the bottom of the valley. Most speculators want to buy a currency just as it turns upward and sell just as it turns down. These are ideals that are seldom, if ever, achieved. One can't recognize the true peaks and valley floors until they're past and then it's too late. The best the beginning speculator can hope to do is catch the trends and ride with them until they turn. An old rule of thumb in futures trading that is well worth repeating is to ride with the winners and dump the losers. Which brings to mind the problem of temperament.

From the brief description of the futures market, it should be apparent that those with lame hearts and weak stomachs should stay out. The ideal speculator will be courageous, tough, and quick. He or she will have the courage to act on a belief of what the market will do. This ideal speculator should be hard enough to take losses without getting discouraged or losing faith in him or herself. And, finally, our perfect speculator must be agile enough to switch positions when the market proves an original belief to be wrong. (The worst mistakes newcomers make are holding losers hoping for a turnaround and selling winners too soon.)

And, of course, our ideal speculator must be wealthy

enough to be able to lose a lot of money invested without being significantly hurt. If you've this temperament, you have the potential to do well. If not, stick to the exchange counter at the airport.

A few words about pricing

Note that for convenience we have been expressing the price of foreign currencies in rounded off numbers. In actual practice, currency quotations are handled slightly differently. The yen, for example, may be expressed in thousandths relative to the value of the U.S. cent—.500 yen to the cent is equivalent to an exchange rate of 200 yen to the dollar. Swiss francs, German marks, British pounds, and so forth are frequently expressed as a decimal carried to the thousandths relative to the dollar value. For example when the Canadian dollar is expressed as .855, its value is 85½ cents to one dollar.

11

Gold, silver, and other precious metal investments

NOT ALL CURRENCY, today, is paper or inexpensive metal coins. There is a different type of currency which many people prefer to invest in instead of dollars, yen, Deutschemarks, and so on. This money consists primarily of gold, both in bullion and coin form. It also includes other types of precious metal such as silver, platinum, and palladium.

This quasi-money is distinct from the currency we've thus far been talking about in two very important ways. First, it normally is not part of the *circulating* currency of any country. We'll explain this further in a moment. Second, it has a dual use both as commodity, in the sense of wheat or pork bellies, and as money.

Many feel that buying gold or other precious metals and holding them over a long period of time is the ultimate investment. I strongly disagree. I'm not saying that big money can't be made in precious metals. It's just that it makes sense to invest in gold when it's hot and in currency when it moves. To simply keep money in one or the other is to overlook investment opportunities.

Before any readers who might be "gold-bugs" begin tearing out pages, let me explain that I do feel that keeping a certain amount of one's wealth at all times in precious metals is a good idea. I also have no objection to "speculating" in gold. I just object to calling it an economic "investment." To see why, let's explore the field a bit. First, which are the precious metals?

Platinum

For years platinum was far and away the most costly of the precious metals. Recently, however, gold has come close to the value of platinum on several occasions. This is probably because of the more active trading in gold. Platinum's properties as a catalyst make it useful in the chemical and petroleum industries. It has a wide variety of other applications in industry.

Platinum is offered for sale in bars. These are usually stamped with a lot number, the fact that the metal is platinum, and the mark of the manufacturing company.

Palladium

Palladium is used as a catalyst in the catalytic converters of modern automobiles. It has additional applications in electronics. It too comes in bars stamped with the word palladium and the mark of the manufacturer.

Silver

Silver may be the most well known of the precious metals. Until 1964 it was used in U.S. coinage. (U.S. coins have contained silver since then, but those are primarily collector coins. See Chapter 12.) It is still widely used in jewelry, in the photographic industry, and in electronics. In addition, it has varied applications in a score of other industries.

Silver is normally available to U.S. citizens in two forms.

The most common form is in bags of U.S. silver coins. These may be dimes, quarters, halves, or dollars, all dated prior to 1964 and containing coins with 90 percent silver in them. The bags normally contain $1,000 in face value. They are sold exclusively for their silver content. The price of such a bag is computed by multiplying the weight of the silver times the price of silver per ounce. The bags normally contain a minimum of 54.5 pounds including the weight of the bag, its seal and tag. Since it is currently legal for U.S. citizens to melt U.S. coinage for its metal content, these bags form a convenient method of buying and selling silver.

Silver coins from several manufacturers are also available. These usually have the word "silver" stamped on the face, the name of the manufacturer, and the silver content. They are bought and sold by weight. The disadvantage of bars over coins is that, although the silver content of the coins is usually assured, it is difficult to know if the bars measure up without an assay.

Gold

Gold is the precious metal that most people think of when considering metal currency. From 1795 until 1933, the United States issued gold coinage for regular circulation. It is currently issued in coin form by at least 45 foreign countries, from Great Britain to Senegal, although it does not circulate. (Foreign countries also issue fiat money which is their circulating currency.)

Gold's other uses include dentistry, electronics, jewelry, and decoration. It can be purchased in both coins and bar forms. The bars normally contain the seal of the manufacturer, the word "gold," and the fineness (gold content). The primary source of new Free World gold is South Africa.

Gold is, without question, the most popular of the precious metals with silver coming in second. Therefore, for the remainder of this chapter we'll deal mainly with gold and, to some extent, with silver.

Gold as a commodity

Gold is both a commodity and a currency. Because in Chapter 1 we pointed out that currency acts like a commodity, some readers might think this statement is redundant. It isn't. Currencies act like commodities; gold *is* a commodity. Consider the true commodity or "physical" value of U.S. dollar bills. They can be used to light a fire, to paper the walls or, in real desperation, to roll around tobacco and create a cigarette. In essence, their true commodity value is the same as for any other piece of paper their size and shape—virtually nothing. Their commodity value, in this sense, is their physical usefulness (not their buying power). That same holds true for higher denomination U.S. coinage. Made of cupro-nickel, our coins contain no more than a few cents of non-precious metal. Their commodity value is negligible. This is not the case for cents, however. Copper prices fluctuate up and down, and at several times have been almost as high as the face value on the cent. (Note: the U.S. does not mint a "penny." That is a denomination formerly minted by Great Britain. The U.S. mints "cents.")

Commodity demand for gold

Gold, on the other hand, has true commodity value, as determined by usefulness. Here are the uses of gold in 1977:

	Metric tons
Carat jewelry	979
Electronics	73
Dentistry	81
Other including industrial and decorative uses	68
Total	1,201

Source: *COINage Magazine*

As a commodity, gold behaves like oil or pork bellies or orange juice. When it is traded on a commodity exchange, hedgers are often composed of gold users from the above-noted industries as well as gold producers such as mining compa-

Gold, silver—precious metal investments

nies. If, however, gold were *only* a commodity, it would not be nearly as costly as it is today.

The worldwide supply and demand for gold from 1948 to 1977 is given on Chart 11A.

CHART 11A   Gold bullion supply and demand—1948-1977

(Metric Tons)

	Free World mine production	Net trade with Communist Bloc	Total supplies	Official purchases or sales	Net private purchases
1948	702	—	702	369	333
49	733	—	733	369	337
1950	755	—	755	288	467
51	733	—	733	235	498
52	755	—	755	205	550
53	755	67	822	404	418
54	795	67	862	595	267
55	835	67	902	591	311
56	871	133	1004	435	569
57	906	231	1137	614	523
58	933	196	1129	605	524
59	1000	266	1266	671	595
1960	1049	177	1226	262	964
61	1080	266	1346	538	808
62	1155	178	1333	329	1004
63	1204	489	1693	729	964
64	1249	400	1649	631	1018
65	1280	355	1635	196	1439
66	1285	-67	1218	-40	1258
67	1250	-5	1245	-1404	2649
68	1245	-29	1216	-620	1836
69	1252	-15	1237	90	1147
1970	1274	-3	1271	236	1035
71	1236	54	1290	-96	1386
72	1183	213	1396	151	1245
73	1121	275	1396	-6	1402
74	1008	220	1228	-20	1248
75	956	149	1105	-15	1120
76	971	412	1383	-70	1453
77	965	401	1366	-241	1607

Source: Chamber of Mines of South Africa

Note from this chart the final figure on the third column, 1,366 metric tons. This represents the total supply of gold from Free World mine production and trade with Communist bloc countries for 1977. When we compare this with total commodity use for 1977, or 1,201 metric tons, we discover that the supply exceeded the *commodity* demand for gold by 165 metric tons. If there were no other demand for gold, this oversupply would cause the price to plummet like a gold bird. (Of course, a dramatic drop in price would result in decreased supplies, eventually stabilizing the price.)

Gold as a currency

There is, of course, an aspect to gold other than its physical commodity usage—its use as a currency. That is a question mark, however. Is gold really a currency? We've already mentioned that for 138 years the U.S. issued gold coins and that about 45 countries today still issue gold coins as legal tender. On the surface this would seem a convincing argument proving that gold is, in fact, a currency. But, appearances can be deceiving. Virtually all of the countries that issue legal tender coinage today, do so for reasons that have nothing to do with currency. The first reason is to create a high-quality coin that collectors will buy. This brings in additional revenue to the country. The second reason applies primarily to gold producing nations, such as South Africa. Here a gold coin is created as a convenient way of selling gold bullion. The South African krugerrand, for example, does not have a denomination (such as half, dollar, quarter, etc.) stamped on it. Rather, it contains exactly one troy ounce of gold and its value is the worth of the gold it contains. If, for example, gold is selling for $200 U.S. an ounce, the krugerrand is worth $200 U.S., plus agent's fees. When gold drops to $190 U.S. an ounce, so does the krugerrand.

A true currency, however, is often defined as coinage that "circulates." By this I mean that it is in common usage in a country. It is used to buy sandwiches, haircuts, newspapers, automobiles, etc. By this definition, there is no real gold currency today.

This argument against gold as a currency is made by some individuals, including many of those who would tax its sale. The argument does have merit, but it fails to account for an unusual property of gold (and silver) that tilts the scale in favoring gold as a currency.

Gold historically

To understand the true currency nature of gold, we must look back to its first use as money. Ancient Egypt did not have money as we know it. But, the Egyptians bartered using amongst other items, small unformed pieces of gold. The first real money was coins created of silver in ancient Lydia and "spades" of bronze in China. Alexander the Great conquered the known world with his sword, then with the Greek silver tetradrachm. Throughout history since then, silver and gold coinage has been issued by every country of substance. And people have always valued these coins.

The value of these coins came only in very small part from government edict. Their value was determined by their exchangeability and their scarcity. People knew and relied on the fact that they could buy things with the coins. And, because there has always been a very limited supply of gold (and silver), they knew governments could not destroy the metal's value by creating huge amounts of new coins.

Of course, governments did try to debase gold coinage. Whenever kings wished to create more money, they put less of the precious metal into the same size coin. This gave rise to a rule which eventually became known as Gresham's law. Briefly, it states that bad money drives good money out of circulation. When a king debased gold coins, the new coins freely circulated, but the people hoarded the older ones because they contained more gold. Gresham's law reflects the population's losing faith in the government and its currency. When U.S. official paper money came into existence, for example, during the U.S. Civil War, it chased gold and silver coins entirely out of circulation.

This belief in gold's exchangeability and its scarcity is why, back in 1933, when the government declared ownership of gold for U.S. citizens to be illegal for any but numismatic (collector) use, it was so hard to gather in the gold coins. People risked stiff criminal penalties to hide it in mattresses and bury it in jars underground. Although almost all was eventually rounded up and melted by the government, the people did demonstrate that they trusted the buying power of gold more than the buying power of paper dollars, at that time. Remember that 1933 was the depth of the depression. The world was in economic chaos. Perhaps the people of the United States were thinking of what happened to the people of Germany only about 15 years earlier, after World War I. At that time the German government's paper money lost all value. It cost 15 million marks to buy a pound of cheese. But gold retained its value. Gold would buy bread and clothes and shelter.

The same holds true today. Survival kits for soldiers who fly missions over or infiltrate hostile territory often include gold, rather than local currency. Why? Because a life might be bargained for with gold, but not with paper.

The value of gold extends to virtually all things. Although today people rarely buy commodities with gold, it is critical to understand that they know they can buy items with gold if they choose to. I would guess that you could go into any Cadillac agency in the country, offer to pay the price of the car in gold, and walk out with the car. Of course, the dealer might want to get an expert opinion on the gold's quality but a purchase could be made. This is even more the case in foreign countries where there hasn't been the lack of gold ownership that there was in the U.S. for over four decades. Of course, people don't do this very often. It is terribly inconvenient. And most people would prefer to spend paper money (Gresham's law). The point is that they know they could do it if they had to.

What all this is hinting at, of course, is that nearly everyone knows that if the worst comes to pass—if there is war, depression, terrible inflation, famine—gold will probably still be valuable. Gold was used long before paper money came into existence. And when paper money is gone, it will be used once again. Gold is outside of our modern civilization. Therefore, when our modern civilization collapses, gold will remain. Gold is the currency of last resort.

This is why I refer to gold as a currency. It always has been and, as far as I can tell, always will be. This is also why there always is a demand for gold totally separate from the demand caused by its usefulness as a commodity. We'll see how this additional demand for gold (and to a lesser degree silver) affects its value in just a moment. But first, the reader should note a very important side-point which derives from this last discussion.

The mystique of gold

Gold is frequently spoken of as a "mysterious" metal. Some believe it has mystical powers. In medieval times royalty ate gold in order to gain better health and economic well-being. Altars to God made of gold are still built in many countries of the world including the United States. All these applications of gold have one thing in common; they make use of the idea that gold has intrinsic value.

Gold has no more intrinsic value than any other currency or commodity. If a government doesn't stand behind its paper currency, it is worthless. If people stop eating pork, pork bellies are a dime a dozen. If people refuse to accept gold as a currency even in times of chaos, gold is no more valuable than granite.

Gold derives its mysterious, mystical aura from a lack of understanding. Many people point to the fact that even when the commodity demand for gold drops (such as when jewelry sales are down), even when it is not really a circulating currency, as is the case today, it still has value. These people then conclude that this value must be intrinsic. Nothing could be further from the truth. The value remains because of the fact that gold is still the currency of last resort for millions of gold hoarders. (In France, which has been overrun in two world wars, it is estimated that *every* French family holds some of its wealth in gold and that nearly 5 percent of the world's supply of gold may be held in France in this manner.) Only if it were possible to eliminate the demand for gold both as a commodity and as a currency of last resort would its value plummet. Then no one would want it simply because no one would have any use for it.

Currency demand for gold—1977

	Metric tons
Medals and "coinlike" items	50
Official coins	136
Private bullion purchases	220
	406

Source: Chamber of Mines of South Africa

Now when we add the currency demand (including investors) to the commodity demand and compare it to the supply we come up with new and startling figures.

Supply/demand for gold—1977

	Metric tons
Commodity demand	1,201
Currency demand	406
Total demand	1,607
Total supply	1,366
Shortfall	-241

In 1977 there were 241 metric tons *less* gold produced than consumed. The figures for shortfall going back to 1948 are given in Chart 11A under "Official purchases or sales." Pay special attention to the years 1973 and onward. Each year the amount of gold used exceeded the total supply by increasing amounts. This trend appears to be continuing into the 1980s.

Gold supply

A word should be said here explaining how use can *exceed* supply. One of the unusual properties of gold is that it is immutable. It does not decay, oxidize, or otherwise change. It can be used over and over again. Perhaps 75 percent or more of all the gold ever mined on this planet is still being used. It is not inconceivable that some of the gold in the bracelets Cleopatra wore has found its way into the ring on your finger or the electrical terminals in your stereo set. What this means is that there is a vast storehouse of gold already mined and made into jewelry or otherwise used. When the price rises sufficiently high, this historical storehouse is tapped. That is why current use can exceed current supply.

Determining gold's price

The price for gold, therefore, is determined in this fashion. Commodity use exerts a demand. Currency use exerts a demand. Production from mining throughout the world, but primarily in South Africa, provides a current supply. Gold melted down from jewelry and from stored bullion provides an historic supply. There are two major sources of demand and two of supply. The point at which they all reach equilibrium is the current price of gold.

These four factors influencing gold prices interact amongst themselves making *giant* fluctuations of gold prices very unlikely.

Since gold has two distinct demands, both of which contribute toward creating price, they tend to moderate one another.

When the commodity demand for gold increases, the currency consumption declines and vice versa. As one lifts prices, the other tends to lower them. The critical point to understand is that for the price of gold to "skyrocket," *both* currency and commodity demands must increase.

An easy way to think of this is a seesaw. When there is an upward or increased demand for gold as a currency, there is a corresponding downward consumption of gold as a commodity. The result is that the price (the center of the seesaw bar) always remains at the same height off the ground.

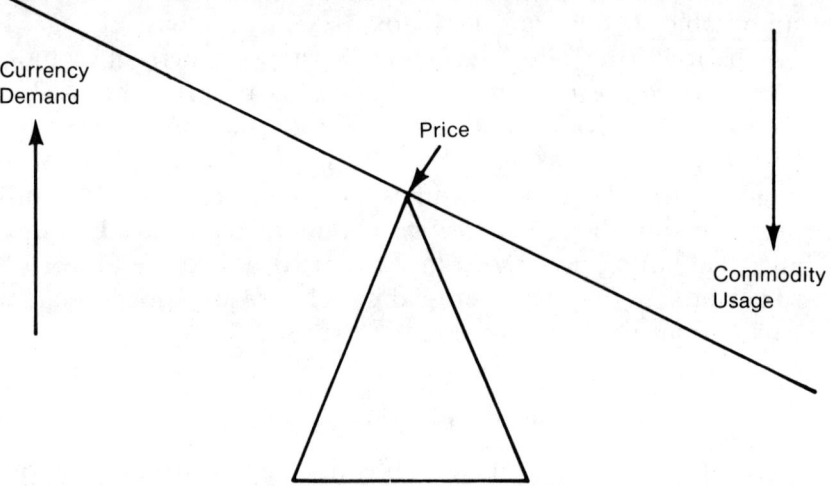

In reality, of course, an increase in demand on one side is normally not entirely offset in the short run by a decrease in consumption on the other side. (In the long run the seesaw effect may even be minimal.) The point is that gold prices, unlike a seesaw bar, can rise.

A similar situation occurs with supply. As we noted, there are two sources of supply, current and historical. In order for prices to increase during an increase in demand, both sources of supply must not simultaneously increase. This is in fact what happens in the short run with current supply. Since the mines are already working to capacity, it is impossible for the existing producers to increase their production of gold. It is not the case, however, with historical supplies.

Most of the historical supply of gold is in government vaults. The amount offered for sale at any given time, therefore, is largely determined by government decision. The United States, for example, still holds about ¼ of the Free World's supply of gold. If it were to suddenly dump *all* of it, the price would surely plummet. As a matter of fact, the United States currently sells very small portions of its gold supply in order to keep the price down. An announcement, for example, in 1978 that the U.S. was going to double its sales quantities drove the price of gold down over $40 an ounce in less than a week.

Investing in gold

An investor wanting to buy gold must take into consideration all the factors we've considered. Sudden economic or political bad news could send gold prices upward, but they will be moderated by less commodity consumption. Sudden increases in demand for commodities could have the same effect. Only a gigantic increase in demand by either commodities or currencies or a simultaneous increase in demand by both could shoot prices substantially higher. But then government sales could cause prices to come right back down.

Only when the U.S. government and the I.M.F. refuse to sell gold (or run out) does the price have a chance to really take off. And even this has another mitigating factor that we have not yet discussed, the Soviet Union.

Russian currency, unlike that of the Free World countries, is not exchangeable. This allows the communist regime to maintain a controlled economy. It does present problems, however, when it comes time to buy goods and services from Free World countries. The Russians solve this by paying for what they want with gold. Since they are probably the world's second largest producer of gold, this is a relatively simple matter for them.

In terms of gold investing, however, their influence is considerable. The Soviets regularly sell metric tons of gold. As the pace of their commodity purchases has increased, so have their gold sales. (Note: temporary swings upward in gold prices are often caused by restrained Soviet sales, temporary dips by increased Soviet gold sales.) Even if the U.S. and the I.M.F. stopped selling gold, the Soviets would not.

This is why the future of gold is not quite as exciting as some of its proponents would like to make it out to be. Increased demands both as a commodity and as a currency have moved the price up in the past. Decreased demand and government sales have moved the price back down. The history of gold price, in fact, has been one of many ups and downs (see Chart 11B).

From this chart it should be apparent that it is possible to "make a killing" on gold, but to do so requires that you be in and out of the market at the right times. Consider the following, assuming that you bought gold for cash (not in the futures market). Were you to have entered the gold market at the end of 1973 (A-see chart) and stayed in until the end of 1976 or three years (D), you would have made virtually nothing. The same is true for the end of 1974 (B) to the end of 1978 (C) or four years. Had you gotten in, however, at the beginning of 1973 (A) and gotten out at the end of 1974 (B), you could have made 67 percent on your money in one year! If you got in at the end of 1978 (C) and got out at the end of 1979 (E), you would have tripled your money in 1 year. On the other hand, by getting in at the end of 1976 (D) and getting out at the end of 1978 (C), you would have made about 70 percent in two years. Staying in from the end of 1973 (A) to the end of 1978 (C) would have yielded you a profit of about 75 percent over five years. (Note: the choice of the end of the year for comparison purposes is simply arbitrary. Any other point during the year might be chosen with similar results.)

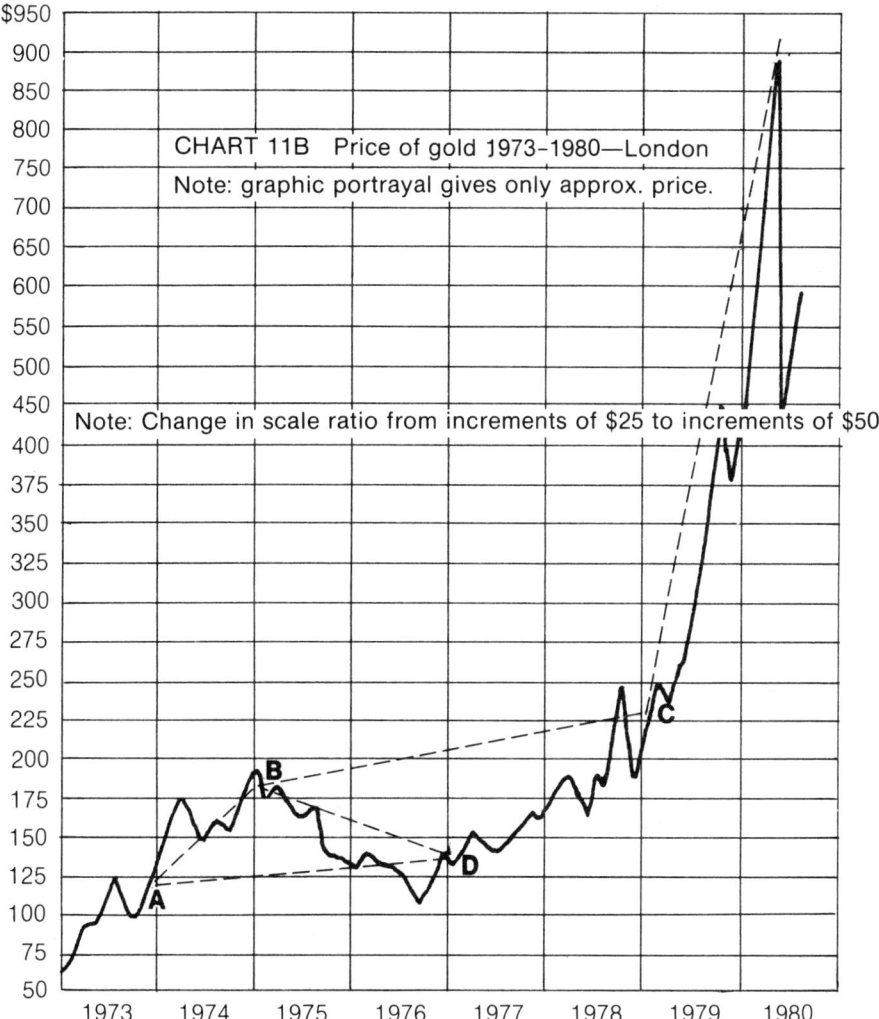

CHART 11B Price of gold 1973–1980—London
Note: graphic portrayal gives only approx. price.
Note: Change in scale ratio from increments of $25 to increments of $50

From this it should be apparent that there is both money to be made and money to be lost in gold. A lot depends on timing. It should be noted that the sharp rise in gold prices ending in 1974 and the subsequent plunge through 1976 could be considered an aberration in the market. Gold was legalized in the U.S. at the end of 1974. Anticipation among speculators ran high that the American public would swarm to gold and this bid the price up prior to legalization. When the public's reaction was cool, the price plunged.

It should also be noted that the steady rise in gold prices since 1976 can at least in small part be attributed to slow but increasing interest in gold by Americans. More and more Americans are purchasing krugerrands, double eagles (U.S. $20 gold pieces usually having numismatic value—see Chapter 12) and British sovereigns. But, as Americans buy gold and provide an enormous new market for the precious metal, government officials are keeping a watchful eye. There is little to prevent them, should the price escalate very far, from suddenly prohibiting gold ownership as they did in 1933.

Is gold a better investment than other currency? Not really. All currency, as we've noted, has its ups and downs. My feeling is that since gold is not really circulating currency in any country, it is more subject to fluctuation. Gold reacts to the dollar similarly to other currencies. When the dollar is down, it tends to be up. But, gold is also down and up at other times as well. It can soar upon announcements of world crisis. It can plunge upon announcement of new government sales.

If you buy gold just before a big price surge and then sell at the peak, it will be very hard to convince you that gold isn't the world's greatest investment. On the other hand, if you buy at the peak and ride it down, you may not look so fondly at the precious metal. All of which to say is that gold, like currencies, can be truly described as a gamble, and sometimes it can be a bit more of a gamble.

Silver as an investment

Now, let's take just a moment to consider silver. Everything we've said about gold, essentially, also applies to silver, with a couple of very important differences.

Unlike gold, silver consumption for years (even decades) has exceeded production. More silver is used every year than is produced. In 1976 mine output of silver in the non-communist countries was about 250 million ounces. Industry and coinage used over 430 million ounces. In 1977 mine output was about 250 million ounces while consumption was 425 million ounces. Consumption remained fairly constant in 1978 while production increased to about 265 million ounces.

This looks rather good for the future of silver. As we've seen, however, appearances can be deceiving. Consider the historic supplies. The U.S. has a currency stock of about 135 million ounces, which every now and then it threatens to sell. The country of India has an estimated three billion ounces of silver, upon which it exerts restrictions. If India were to suddenly unleash that silver, the price would certainly plummet. Finally, there is the fact that most silver commodity usage goes to photographic purposes. It has been rumored from time to time that new scientific breakthroughs will eliminate the use of silver here. If and when this happens, a severe reduction in demand will undercut prices.

The bright picture we were painting for silver suddenly looks tarnished. But, there is yet another side to silver. Most of the present shortage of silver (difference between current production vs. demand) is made up from historic stocks of coins and from silver scrap (reclaimed from photographic processes and elsewhere). The amount of silver available *from these sources* is diminishing each year, putting upward pressure on its price.

Putting this all together we come up with the following conclusions. *If* the U.S. doesn't sell its silver stockpile; *If* India doesn't dump silver; *If* no new sources of historic supplies or scrap are found; *If* consumption continues at its present pace (there is some indication that even the use of silver in collector coins is diminishing); *then* the price of silver could go higher, much higher.

All of which is to say that if I wanted to take a real gamble, I'd bet on silver. It's a longshot that might win the race, or break a leg in the stretch.

12

Should you try collectible currency?

WHEN IS A DOLLAR not a dollar? When it's a collector coin. Then it's not a dollar because it may be worth far more than the value stamped on its face.

Thus far we have ignored the world of "numismatics" or collector coins and currency. But, it is an area which deserves much more attention for reasons that we shall soon see.

Many people shy away from collector coins for a variety of reasons. Some feel that you must be an expert in order to profit. Others feel that the market is too small and buying and selling is difficult. Still others believe that the large profits reported by some within the field are puffed up. I can tell you that all these fears are exaggerated. For ten years I was editor of *COINage*, the world's largest circulation coin magazine. Although company policy forbade my owning rare coins myself, I witnessed many others making fortunes—sometimes, those entirely new to the field.

Let's examine the objections that people may have to

Should you try collectible currency? 177

collectible coins one at a time, beginning with an area that usually has the most interest—profit. Is there really much profit to be made collecting coins?

I have seen writers in the field pick this coin or that and point to a dramatic increase in value, perhaps 1,000 percent or more, over a couple of years. I am not much impressed by such arguments and, if you're an astute reader, you shouldn't be either. I want to know not how one coin or a specially selected series of coins is doing, but how the overall field is doing. This very curiosity led to an interesting experiment we did at *COINage* several years ago. But, before we get into that, let's consider the costs that are going to be involved in any coinage investment.

Storage

First, there is the cost of storage or insurance. Just as you must pay a high premium to insure a rare and valuable painting, so too must you pay such a premium to insure a rare coin collection (when insurance is available). Many collectors finesse this problem by keeping their collection locked safely away in a safety deposit box in a bank. Then there is only the cost of the box (although this means the collector can't show off his collection—a real problem for a true hobbyist).

Lost leverage

Second, there is the lack of leverage. When you buy a commodity, as we've seen, very often you need only come up with 5 percent or less of the value as a security deposit. Even when you buy a home, typically you need only come up with 20 percent of the value. When you buy a rare coin you must come up with 100 percent of the value in cash. This lack of leverage is expressed by substitution. If we figure that 20 percent is the minimum leverage figure, then 80 percent of what you put in coins could, in some other investments, be spent elsewhere or at least kept in a savings account. This means that for each dollar you spend on a rare coin, you would be wise to calculate how much interest you are losing by not investing that same dollar in some other field. (It might be argued that borrowed money in real estate, which provides the leverage, also requires interest payment. Therefore, if your alternative is a real estate investment, disregard the following few paragraphs.) This is measured quite simply by taking 80 percent of your rare coin investment and calculating how much interest you would have earned on that money by keeping it instead in a time account in a bank.

Selling costs

Third and last, most people are required to buy retail and sell wholesale. Consequently, when a price is quoted in an article or book demonstrating how much coins have appreciated in value, it may be inappropriate since it usually shows retail to retail. Retail to wholesale is somewhat less. How much less is open to discussion. Some people can sell for retail through coin clubs or by advertisements placed by themselves in coin publications. Others simply turn the coin over to a dealer. Overall, we might guess that as much as 20 percent of the retail value is lost when a coin is sold.

Now, having made clear what the costs of collecting are, let's consider the potential profit. An experiment was done at *COINage* magazine in 1973-74. The editors selected 20 key coins. (A key coin is one that typifies an entire series. It usually is a well-known coin.) These included cents, nickels, dimes, quarters, halves, dollars, and proof sets. The idea was to get a feeling for how the entire field was progressing, either upward or downward, in terms of coin prices.

Thereafter, each month we plotted the retail price of these coins as reported by dealers across the country. Over the course of years, none of the coins turned out to be "super-hot" purchases and perhaps ¼ of them turned out to be losers—coins that never lost value, but never gained much value either. We felt throughout that these coins were indeed representative of coin prices overall.

In January of 1974 the total value of all 20 coins at retail was $3,262.25. Five years later in January of 1979 the total value of these 20 coins at retail was $10,213.75. (We didn't buy or sell the coins—only checked prices.)

How much profit would someone entering the field in 1974 and buying these 20 well-known key coins have made over the course of the ensuing five years? Here's the calculation. First, the costs:

1.) Storage and insurance: $10 a year for a safety deposit box in a bank = $50.

2.) Lost interest because of no leverage (80% x $3,262.25 x 5% interest per year) = roughly $750.00

3.) 20% deducted from retail at the time of selling = $2,042.75

Total costs of owning the 20 key coins:

Storage and insurance =	$ 50.00
Lost interest =	750.00
20% off retail =	2,042.75
Total	2,842.75

When the cost of $2,842.75 is deducted from the retail price in 1979 we find that the actual selling price after costs is $7,371. When this is compared with our purchase price of $3,262.25 we find that the profit over five years on the coins was $4,108.75 or 125 percent. That works out to be about 18 percent a year.

Several things should be carefully noted about this example. The first is that the most conservative approach possible has been taken toward calculating profit. Second, the coins chosen were in no way unusual. They were, in fact, well known to most expert numismatists. Finally, a shrewd collector having a choice of 20 coins might very well have picked out one or two

180 Buying and selling currency for profit

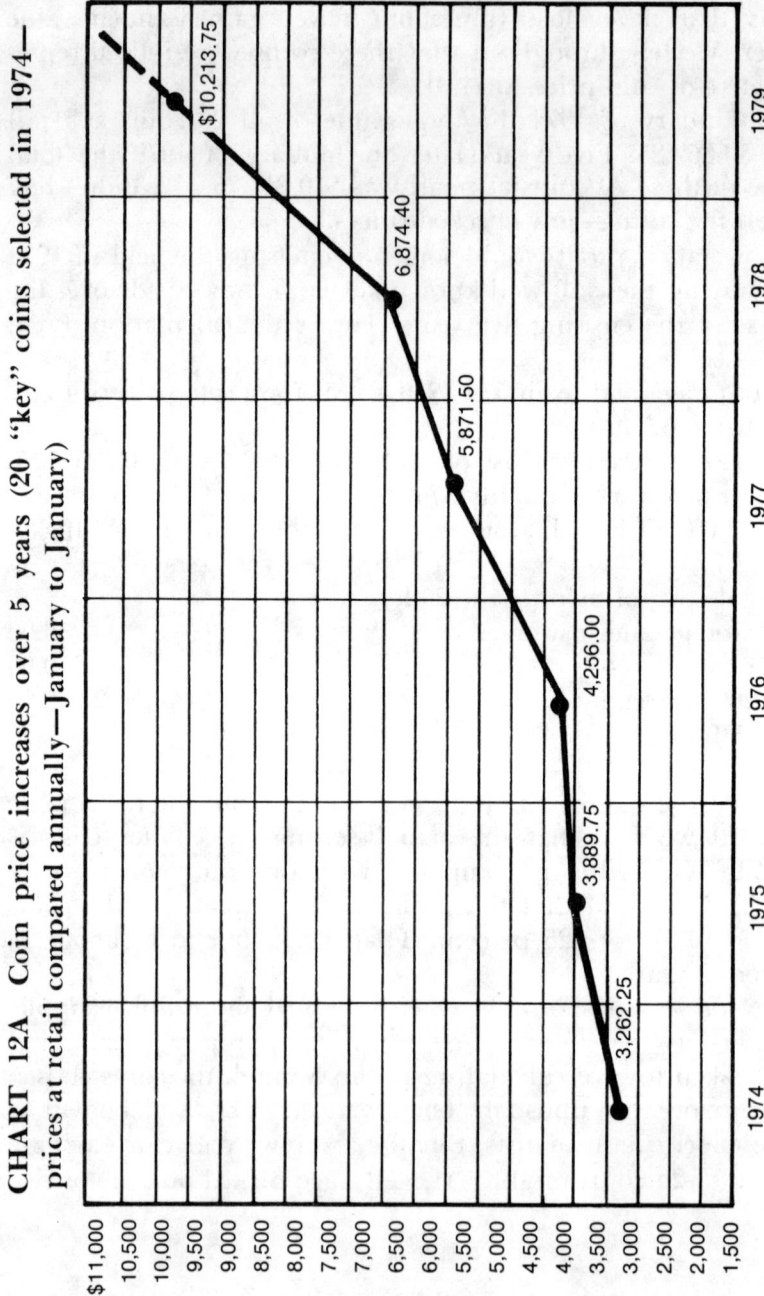

CHART 12A Coin price increases over 5 years (20 "key" coins selected in 1974—prices at retail compared annually—January to January)

that might have skyrocketed in value during the period and this could have sent the profit picture up much higher.

There you have an indication of the potential profit to be made by coin investing. (Readers should note, of course, that no guarantee or assurance is given that these 20 coins or any others will show appreciation in value at any time in the future.) Note: Coin prices tend not to be volatile. There are increases and plateaus, but very few price decreases in recent years.

Let's consider another objection to collector coins—that the field is too small. It has been reliably estimated that there are more than eight million coin collectors in the United States alone. There are at least four national monthly magazines, three of which are widely sold on newsstands. There are three major newspapers; two are weeklies, which cater exclusively to the field. There are coin dealers in almost every city in the country, many linked together by several nationwide teletype-computer systems giving instant pricing information. There are thousands of books on the subject. (See Chapter 11 for several recommended ones.) Coin collecting is not a small field and there is no problem finding buyers or sellers for material, provided the price is right.

Finally, there is the matter of judging coins. This objection centers on the fact that unless you're an expert in the field you can't recognize good material when you see it. I've saved this argument for last because it warrants careful scrutiny.

The value of numismatic coins is based on three things. The first is demand. While the entire field has a demand curve, some people tend to like one coin more than another for no apparent reason. Each coin, therefore, has its own demand curve within a curve. This is only to say that some coins are popular while others are not. It takes only a passing acquaintance with the hobby to discover which coins are traditionally popular and which are currently undergoing a fad of desirability. Just read the coin publications, talk to dealers, and you'll quickly know.

The second determination of value is rarity—how many of the coins actually exist. In the case of known rarity, such as the 1913 Liberty Head nickel, the price is very high—in the hundreds of thousands of dollars for each specimen. In cases of guessed rarity such as the 1909 S VDB cent, where there could be as many as 484,000 coins out there, the price is in the hundreds of dollars per specimen. In most cases the total mintage can be found quickly. What's difficult or even impossible to know is how many coins of those minted were lost, worn out, or destroyed. Which is to say, how many are actually left? There are as many opinions here as there are experts, and being a beginner is no handicap.

The last determination of value is quality. It is in this area that a careless beginner can truly be hurt.

Coins are judged on condition just as are diamonds or rare paintings. There is a relatively new system that has been adopted by the American Numismatic Association and which is widely used. It rates coins on a scale from MS-70 on downward to zero.

"MS" is short for "Mint State." It simply refers to the condition of a coin just as it leaves the press at the mint when it is "MS-70"—shiny, no scratches or other imperfections. MS-60 indicates Uncirculated or that the coin has made it from the mint to the bank to a collector with a little wear along the way. MS-40 indicates it has some wear but is still in Extremely Fine condition. MS-12 indicates Fine condition. MS-4 is Good condition. (The descriptive words are from an earlier system of coin grading.) There is another whole type of coin called "Proof," which is made exclusively for collectors by a different procedure and which usually commands the highest prices.

At this point you may be tempted to look at your pocket change and pick out coins in various conditions. Don't do it. Most collector coins are MS-40 or higher. Coins that are graded lower than MS-60 drop off dramatically in value. Most coins in pocket change are so badly marred that they are below MS-20 on the scale.

Should you try collectible currency? 183

The point is that it takes an expert to tell. Most beginners can look at an MS-20 or Very Fine coin and swear it looks perfect. To the untrained eye, it very well may. But, an expert knows how to look for lack of detail on eagle feathers on a reverse. Or an almost invisible line worn off the nose on the obverse (front or face). I repeat, if you're not an expert, don't try to judge coin condition.

As might be guessed, quality is a great determiner of price. If you buy a coin at a price for MS-60, then go to sell and find that you graded it wrong and it's only MS-40, you could not only lose your anticipated profit, but much of your original investment.

How, then, does a beginner successfully grade coins? The answer is he or she doesn't. If you're not an expert, find someone who is and rely on his or her advice. That's the way most rare paintings, diamonds, and other such commodities are sold.

How do you find an expert? Most dealers, though not all, are reputable. They want your business over a long period of time. They hope that years hence you'll sell back to them the very same coin that today they sell to you. They grade carefully and honestly. One way to invest in coins is to find a dealer whom you can trust. Your own judgment will have to guide you.

There are also coin clubs all over the country. These clubs hold shows at which there may be coin pricing tables. For no fee or just a nominal one, an expert will grade a coin there for you. Clubs also often have resident experts who can help grade coins at regular meetings.

Finally, The American Numismatic Association will both grade the quality of a coin and issue a certificate of authenticity (if, of course, it isn't counterfeit). The grading and authenticity certificate are widely accepted; it is a coin's pedigree. The Association's address is given at the end of this chapter. (Do not send coins through the mail until you've first contacted the association for the proper mailing procedure.)

One last caution is in order and that has to do with counterfeits. Like anything valuable (including $20 bills), rare coins are occasionally counterfeited. Every buyer must be aware of this possibility. This means you should be particularly wary of anyone trying to sell you a rare coin at far less than quoted retail value.

Finally, in all honesty I must say that a beginner entering numismatics with an eye *strictly* to making a profit takes a certain risk. You might get stuck with a misgraded or phony coin. You might pay a higher than retail price and, of course, there's always that chance that the coins you buy simply won't appreciate in value.

Of course, there is risk to every investment. And I'm not sure the risks in numismatics are greater than anywhere else. As I noted in the introduction of this book, there are no guarantees in life except the proverbial death and taxes.

There is one way I have observed, however, which eliminates most of the pitfalls of coin collecting. Give up the idea of entering the field for strictly investment purposes. Take up coin collecting as a hobby. It's not an unpleasant hobby. Learning history from coins can be fascinating. Over a period of time, through small purchases, you'll learn good coins from bad. You'll take the knocks that beginners in all fields receive. But, since you'll like what you're doing, they won't hurt so much. And after a while, you'll suddenly find that you're your own expert. I have never known anyone who purchased coins in this fashion and held them for a *long* period of time, say 10 to 20 years, who didn't make an enormous profit upon their sale.

For further help in collecting, you may contact the American Numismatic Association, P.O. Box 2366, Colorado Springs, CO 80901. They have a wide range of programs and services including an extensive lending library.

Appendix
Sources of additional information

A SERIOUS INVESTOR in currency will want to obtain the most up-to-date and accurate information. The following list includes pamphlets, news publications, periodicals, and books that I have found helpful. The list, of course, should not be considered complete, but rather as a starting point. I have specifically chosen material that is readable and easily understood. Where possible, I have indicated the most recent price (many publications are free and I have noted this where applicable). Prices do change, however, and to be sure of receiving desired material in as short a time as possible, I suggest you either call the publisher for a recent price quote, or include extra money.

Chicago Mercantile Exchange
International Monetary Market
444 West Jackson Boulevard
Chicago, Ill. 60606

The following publications are available upon request from the Chicago Mercantile Exchange:

Trading in Tomorrows—Explains how a commodity exchange works and gives brief explanations of futures trading.

Before You Speculate—"A distillation of the thoughts and experience of recognized authorities . . . in commodity futures trading." Six essays.

Futures Trading in International Currencies—Gives conditions for trade as well as a break-down of the economies of the countries involved.

Trading in Silver Coin Futures
Futures Trading in Gold
Understanding Futures in Foreign Exchange
Understanding Trading in Gold Futures
A Guide to Silver Coin Future Trading
International Monetary Market Weekly Publication—Charts price movements in foreign currency, gold, T-Bill futures. Includes a weekly monetary review.

CM Report
Chamber of Mines of South Africa
5 Holland Street
Johannesburg, S.A.

A monthly publication that prints vital statistics in the gold field. Includes articles on up-to-date trends as well as new developments in mining and usage.

COINage magazine
17337 Ventura Blvd.
Enrico, CA 91316
Annual subscription $11.00

A monthly publication that deals with all aspects of numismatics. Includes numerous investment articles on coins, currency, gold, silver, ingots, and metals. Also features articles of hobby interest. World's largest circulation coin magazine.

Commodity Perspective
327 S. La Salle St.
Chicago, IL 60604

Weekly publication which charts prices of many commodities, currencies, and metals. Issues often run to sixty pages or more. One year subscription price is over $200.

Deak-Perera
Deak and Co., Inc.
Deak-Perera Building
29 Broadway
New York, NY 10006

The largest and oldest foreign exchange company in the western hemisphere. They have more than 50 offices worldwide and can handle foreign exchange in virtually any currency. They also offer a recorded price quoting service. Offices, besides New York, are located in Stamford, Connecticut; Washington, D.C; Miami, Florida; Honolulu, Hawaii; and Chicago, Illinois, and at the international area of several major airports.

Federal Reserve Bulletin
Division of Administrative Services
Board of Governors of the Federal Reserve System
Washington, DC 20551

Monthly: $20 per year. A monthly publication which includes vital statistics on the monetary performance of the U.S. economy. Also includes many articles of current interest on the monetary system.

Federal Reserve Chart Book
Publication Services
Division of Administrative Services
Board of Governors of the Federal Reserve System
Washington, D.C. 20551

Published quarterly: $7 per year. Filled with graphic portrayals of the U.S. economy with special headings for: Monetary Aggregates, Economic Activity, Funds Raised and Supplied, Federal Finance, State and Local Finance, Corporate Finance, Household Finance, Mortgage Debt, Financial Institutions, Stock Market and Interest Rates, U.S. International Transactions, Foreign Interest Rates, and Exchange Rates.

A subscription, in the past, has also entitled the subscriber to the annual *Historical Chart Book*.

Financial Bulletin of the Federal Reserve Bank of St. Louis
P.O. Box 442
St. Louis, MO 63166

Available upon request: published monthly. Includes charts of monetary activity in the U.S., plus a highly informative ½-page summary of recent banking activity. This may be the most up-to-date information available.

The Gold News
Suite 1140
1001 Connecticut Ave.
Washington, DC 20036

Contains statistics on gold use and production as well as articles on gold applications. Monthly. Also offers *Modern Gold Coinage*, a large looseleaf book of some 50 pages listing gold coinages by country. Includes size, weight, percent of gold, and number of coins in issue. Extremely helpful aid.

A Guidebook of U.S. Coins (The Red Book)
by R.S. Yeoman
Western Publishing Co.
Racine, WI 53404

Available in most bookstores. Under $5.00. Gives the current numismatic price of all U.S. coins. It also includes some pertinent information on coins and collecting. It is considered the "Bible" of numismatics. Updated annually.

Handbook of U.S. Coins (The Blue Book)
by R. S. Yeoman
Western Publishing Co.
Racine, WI 53404

Available in larger bookstores. Under $5.00. Lists the dealer price for coins.

High Profits from Rare Coin Investments
by Q. David Bowers
Bowers and Ruddy Galleries, subsidiary of General Mills
6922 Hollywood Blvd.
Los Angeles, CA 90028

One of the best coin investment books on the market.

Inflation
John Calder (Publishers) Ltd.
18 Brewer St.
London, W1R 4AS England

Under $10, 192 pages. A record of inflation from ancient times to the present in Europe. Gives a keen insight into the European understanding of inflation. Includes essays by Thomas Mann, Walt Rostow, and Michael Jefferson.

International Monetary Fund
Write to: Secretary
International Monetary Fund
Washington, DC 29431

The Fund publishes a wide variety of books giving far-ranging international information on nearly all countries. An invaluable aid for currency investors:

International Financial Statistics

Monthly publication, $35 per year, single issue—$3.50. This is the "Bible" of international financial study. Gives hundreds of pertinent facts and information on countries. Widely used by bankers and financial investors.

Direction of Trade

Monthly publication, 12 issues, and an annual in book form, $16. Single copies for $1.50, Annual for $4.50. Includes the latest information on each country's direction of trade with comparisons of previous year.

Balance of Payments Yearbook

BOP statistics for the 110 members of the IMF. Monthly information in booklet-form plus book-form annual. Subscription price is $20.

Other publications for specific interests are available.

Money and Inflation—A Monetarist Approach
by J. Huston McCulloch
Academic Press, Inc.
111 Fifth Ave.
New York, NY

Under $5.00, 123 pages. Gives a very quick, but very effective explanation of inflation in terms most lay pople can easily understand. A highly readable book.

New York Mercantile Exchange
Dept. of Research and Education
Four World Trade Center
New York, NY 10048

The following publications are available upon request from the New York Mercantile Exchange:

NYME—explains the exchange and what it deals in.
International Currency Futures—gives rules of trade
The ABC's of Commodities
Monthly Report
Statistical Yearbook

Official A.N.A. Grading Standards for U.S. Coins
by Ken Bressett and Abe Kosoff
Western Publishing Co.
Racine, WI 53404

Price: $5.95. Gives descriptions for thirteen standard grading conditions for United States coins.

The Silver Institute Letter
1001 Connecticut Ave. NW
Washington, DC 10036

A monthly publication which contains information on silver, primarily for industry use. Includes statistics on silver production and consumption. Also features many articles on unusual uses of silver.

The Wall Street Journal
22 Cortlandt St.
New York, NY 10007

Published daily except Saturday and Sunday. Available in regional editions. This paper is a real financial education in itself.

Possibly the most reliable, up-to-date information available on all markets, including both spot and future prices for commodities and currencies. Short as well as occasional in-depth articles probe the fields. Many are written by knowledgeable experts in the area.

In addition to the sources indicated above, most large banks maintain substantial International Departments. Economists employed by these banks constantly research economic indicators for bank use. In many cases these banks will allow their customers to pick the brains of these experts, either by giving out printed information, or by actual conversations. The hitch is that they rarely will do it for someone simply walking in off the street. Usually you must be a good customer (have a substantial bank balance). If you can get access to this information, it may be the latest and most easily digestible.

To get instant quotes on currency and metals prices, I suggest you strike up a friendly relationship with a good commodities broker. Other sources of this information include banks, as noted above, and currency exchange offices.

Index

A

American Numismatic Association (ANA), 183-84
Arbitrageurs, 150

B

Balance of payments, 77-80
Balance of payments chart, 69
Banking, 102-8
Barter, 19
Blue country, 31-33
Borrowing, 25
Bretton Woods, 66-67

C

Cash, 95-98
Chamber of Mines of South Africa, 186
Chicago Mercantile Exchange, 185
Coins, 176-84
   counterfeits, 184
   demand, 181
   investment analysis, 178-81
   judging quality, 181-83
   leverage, 177
   Mint State (MS), 182
   rarity, 182
   selling costs, 178
   size of hobby, 181
   storage, 177
COINage magazine, 186
Commodities
   brokers, 136-37, 139
   markets, 135-36
   planning investments, 137-38
Commodity futures, 135-58
   at-the-market order, 154
   commission, 153
   day-order, 154
   delivery, 4, 142-43
   deposit, 4-5, 141, 143-48
   hedging, 142, 146, 148-50
   limit order, 154
   limits, 144
   long position, 143, 150-51
   maintenance margin, 144
   market, 3-5
   offsetting contract, 142

193

open order, 154
opening contract, 141
peaks and valleys, 157-58
pricing, 158
risk, 147
short position, 146-47, 150-51
speculators, 145-48
stop-loss order, 153
technical analysis, 154-57
temperment, 157, 158
Consumer Price Index (CPI), 48-49
Creating private money, 104-16
Currency
　circulating, 159, 164, 165
　coin supply chart, 96
　trends chart, 89
Current account, 70-71, 73-75
Current account chart, 74

D

Deak-Perera, 187
Demand
　accounts, 97
　curve, 12
　demand/supply chart, 17
　demand/supply curve, 16
　increase chart, 13
　manufactured goods, 119-21
　orange juice, 10-18
　　chart, 11
　static, 10, 12-13
Deutschemark I(DM), 1-3
Dollar
　devaluation, 71-75
　dumping, 114-16
　gap, 67
　glut, 67

E

Economic
　announcements, 91
　independence, 82
　indicators (list), 6-7
　surprise, 91
Efficiency
　automobile manufacturing, 62-63
　charts
　　Canada, 40
　　England, 39
　　France, 37
　　Germany, 36
　　Japan, 41
　　Switzerland, 38
　　United States, 35, 42
　production, 33-43
England (economic analysis), 127-28
Equilibrium, 76-77
Establishing value, 31-33
European
　Monetary System (EMS), 125-27
　"snake," 125
Exchange of currency, 1-3
　inflation, 49, 60
　origin, 31-32
　rate, 2
　Yen, 29-31

F

Federal Deposit Insurance Corporation, 109
Federal Reserve System, 100, 103, 108-10, 187
Fiat currency, 20, 95

Food (as weapon), 86
Foreign
  aid, 68-70
  currency price of U.S. dollar, 73
  currency values, 1975-1978
    Canada, 45
    England, 45
    France, 44
    Germany, 43
    Japan, 46
    Switzerland, 44
    United States, 46
  purchases, 29-30
Forward Pricing, 140-43
Fractional reserve banking, 107-8

G

Germany (economic analysis), 124-27
Golads, 151-58
Gold, 161-75
  commodity, 162-63
  confiscation, 166
  currency, 50-51
  currency demand/supply chart, 168
  dollar backing, 66-75
  fixed rate, 50-51, 67
  historically, 165-67
  investment, 171-74
  mystique, 167, 169
  origin, 20
  price, 169-72
  price history chart, 173
  Soviet Union supply, 171-72
  supply, 169-71
  supply/demand chart, 163
  use chart, 162

Gold News, The, 188
Government controls, 122-23
Gresham's Law, 165
Guidebook of U.S. Coins, A, (The Red Book), 188

H-I

Handbook of U.S. Coins (The Blue Book), 189
High Profits From Rare Coin Investments, 189
Inflation, 118-21
Inflation rate charts,
  Canada, 55
  England, 54
  France, 53
  Germany, 52
  Japan, 57
  Mexico, 59
  Switzerland, 56
  United States, 58
Interest rates (international), 64-65
Interest rate parity (IRP), 149
International banking, 110-14
International Monetary Fund, 7, 66-75, 171, 189
Intervention, 6, 75-80, 115-16, 133-34
Iran, 87

J-L

Japan (economic analysis), 129-30
Law of One Price, 61-62
Law of Supply, 15
Leakage, 107
Liquidity, 108

M

Margin. *See* Commodity futures, deposit.
Mexico (economic analysis), 130-33
Money
   demand for, 23-25
   demand chart, 27
   demand/supply, 27
   inflation, 190
   need chart, 24
   original, 165
   price, 25-28
   supply, 95-98
   supply chart, 99
   village (example), 19-23
Multiplier effect, 113
M-1, 97
M-2, 97-98
M-3, 98

N

National debt, 98-102
   chart, 101
New York Mercantile Exchange, 190

O

Official ANA Grading Standards for U.S. Coins, 191
Oil
   currency, 84-88
   currency conversion, 84-86
   inflation, 51, 84
   Mexico, 132-33
   productivity, 84
   United States, 118-19
Oil Producing and Exporting Countries (OPEC), 83-88, 90-91

P

Palladium, 169
Phil, 3-5
Platinum, 160
Price inflation, origin, 20-23
Price, optimum, 16
Principle of substitution, 11
Purchasing Power Parity (PPP), 60-64

R

Red country, 31-33
Risk (influence on money price), 26

S

Saudi Arabia, 84-85
Scarcity, 10
Seignorage, 96
Shipping charges, 61-62
Silver, 95, 160-61, 174-75
Silver Institute Letter, The, 191
Smithsonian meeting, 71
Special Drawing Rights (SDR), 73
Spot rate, 141
Supply and demand, 9-28
Supply curve, 14-18
   price, 10
Susan B. Anthony dollar, 96
Swiss franc (SF), 3-5
Switzerland (economic analysis), 128-29

T

Time deposits, 97-98
Trade, 31-33
Trade dollars, 50
Trade with Japan, 60-64, 76
Treasury bills, 100

U

Unemployment, 120-21
United States
   balance of payments, 118
   economic analysis, 117, 123
   foreign investments, 68
   gold stock chart, 72
   natural resources, 82-83
   productivity, 117, 118
   trade chart, 80

V-W

Volatility, 90-93
Wall Street Journal, 191
Wholesale Price Index, 49